BUT NOT ON
OUR BLOCK

Also by
Henry Viscardi, Jr.

THE ABILITIES STORY '67
THE SCHOOL '64
A LETTER TO JIMMY '62
A LAUGHTER IN THE LONELY NIGHT '61
GIVE US THE TOOLS '59
A MAN'S STATURE '52

But not on our Block '72

The Phoenix Child '74

BUT NOT ON OUR BLOCK

by
HENRY VISCARDI, JR.

Paul S. Eriksson, Inc.
New York

This book is respectfully dedicated to De Witt Wallace who has always walked in gentleness and whose devotion and dedication to disabled children have made him truly a patron of mankind.

ILLUSTRATIONS

PREFACE

||||||||||||||||||||||||||||||||||||||||||||||||

This is a personal story—the story of a conflict that continues, that has not been won and may not be won in my lifetime. It is a story not only of the people whose cause I willingly serve but also one of new developments and attitudes reaching across our whole nation. These patterns have become a challenge to all of us, in the sprawling cities, jungles and ghettos, and in burgeoning new suburban America as well.

I believe that everyone needs to know and to understand the meanings and implications in this record of our responsibility and (sometimes our lack of responsibility) as citizens. Yet at the surface level it concerns a rather simple matter—the construction of a handsome new building to provide a gymnasium, learning center and a cafeteria for some two hundred severely handicapped children, all of whom were homebound because of disability and could never have gone to any school had we not set one up for them at our Human Resources Center in Albertson, Long Island.

As always before, with every step along our way, we had to face opposition from some elements in the com-

munity around us. In general, the opposition came
from those who did not want us there at all, who
simply did not want a Center like ours in their picket-
fence paradise, who did not want to look at the crippled children in our school.

It is an old story, as familiar to the disabled as to
other minorities who have to cope with closed minds
and closed hearts. Prejudice is an ugly word. Real
reasons can always be camouflaged behind seemingly
plausible reasons, grounds for opposition. But back of
whatever grounds are claimed other forces are almost
always at play. Superstition that dates back to primitive times, ignorance, insecurity, frustration, fear.
The official reason is never that the skin is black, the
religion wrong, or the children deformed.

In telling this story, with all its personal as well as
social implications, I believe I am also providing a
front line report on what is happening in many other
areas of suburban America. I am talking about the
tentacles of fear and distrust, of a festering new personal isolationism that has become a hallmark of too
many of the new suburbs in our country today.

I never accepted for a moment the idea that all or
even a majority of the people around us have been
against our Center for educational research for the
disabled, our internationally known workshop, Abilities, Inc., as well as our research foundation and the
school. There is overwhelming evidence that most of
the community supports our work. But it is also true,
unfortunately, that the affirmative voices of individual
average citizens are hard to hear above the raucous

shouts of organized protest leadership and their eager, highly vocal lawyers.

I believe, moreover, that what I am writing here is much more than what has happened to one group, one center such as ours, one school for special children like ours. It is rather a report of what we of the 1970's are doing to our own communities, urban and suburban, to our own neighbors, to ourselves.

I write of these perilous areas because I am convinced we must begin to understand them—and to change their directions—before we are too late.

Henry Viscardi, Jr.

Albertson, N.Y.
October, 1971

CONTENTS

xi

PROLOGUE

||||||||||||||||||||||||||||||||||||||||||||||||||||||||||

The town of Albertson, Long Island, in the midst of
which is located our Human Resources Center with
its workshop and school, is not really a town at all. It
is rather a community, a neighborhood, a postal district, similar to numerous other Long Island communities which merge into larger townships, yet still
maintain their unique identity, even if in name only.

Technically, the community of Albertson lies
within the incorporated jurisdiction of the town of
North Hempstead, a sprawling compendium of communities reaching from Glen Cove and Great Neck on
the north, halfway across to the Island's south shore.
It is part of a familiar process dating back to Long
Island's earliest days: communities and neighborhoods spring up, eventually band together into larger
suburban centers, and yet cling to their past and their
traditions. Our location was first known as Searingtown. Searingtown Road is still one of the major thor-
oughfares in the area. It was an obscure village in its
early years—a handful of houses surrounded by farms

and foliage, dogwood, pine and undergrowth and wide green fields.

When we—a small group of other disabled persons and I—began Abilities in the early 1950's we set up shop not in Albertson but in a rented garage a few miles distant in West Hempstead. This was the original Abilities, Inc., established to demonstrate that handicapped people even with severe disabilities could learn to work, to produce, to earn their own way.

I myself knew well from my own personal experience the difficulties of striving for such goals. Born with twisted stumps for legs, growing up on the upper West Side of Manhattan, I had to learn to struggle each step of the way on those streets—through school, through college. Later, after I had artificial limbs, I began a successful career in industry. This career I gave up for goals I considered infinitely more important—working to help handicapped men and women find not made work, not charity, but jobs, real jobs, in which they could have pride and independence and self-respect.

Five of us began in that garage with a total altogether of five good arms and one good leg. Ultimately we built an operation employing more than four hundred handicapped men and women who produced on a level of individual proficiency and precision matching or excelling the production of the nondisabled.

We were meeting a need, pioneering in a long neglected area of society, and we were growing swiftly.

It was soon apparent that we had to have larger quarters, and as the work load expanded we decided to build our own plant. I assumed the job of raising the funds and set out to find the location. That was how we discovered the nearby community of Albertson.

The property we bought in Albertson could hardly have been described at the time of purchase as a garden spot in the community. It was, in fact, part swamp and part town dump. Half a century earlier, it had been part of a farm; fragments of the original farmhouse foundation were found on our property, along with a few gaunt fruit trees.

Many Albertson residents welcomed us; some in the immediate neighborhood, however, were strongly opposed to us from the beginning. They did not want us or our crutches and wheelchairs in the midst of Albertson's sylvan beauty. Yet the truth was that the property we purchased had been lying there as an unused wasteland where people living nearby walked their dogs and dumped discarded refrigerators, mattresses, radios, and junk hauled out of attic or garage.

Our original parcel was seven-and-a-half acres. Before we took over, most of the tract was so swampy that it had become a breeding ground for insects. Ducks nested here. The entire original land was zoned for shopping center use, not for residential use. The material dumped on the ground by residents had turned the place into a festering sore. Instead of allowing this pollution to continue, we engaged an architect to design and build a magnificent building in a setting of driveways, landscaping, carefully planned trees, shrubbery and flowers.

We had to bring in tons of fill to turn this land into a truly lovely and usable spot. Low-lying areas had to be drained, and extensive grading was done. In ensuing years we have added several other parcels to this tract; the whole now totals twenty acres. Part of the land is on relatively high ground and a small brook now runs through part of it during the wet seasons of spring or after a heavy rainfall.

In 1957, when we first began to build in our new location, the flight of city dwellers had already begun, and Albertson, with the surrounding areas of Williston, Roslyn, New Hyde Park and other communities, was already an established new suburban area. Yet much of Albertson was still wooded and there were only a dozen or so houses close to us. Even then, however, the protesters were organized and ready. They came with their civic association to oppose our first building application before the North Hempstead Board of Zoning Appeals.

They wanted to continue to walk their dogs on this land even though we explained that the property was now ours; we had purchased it. They challenged our right to cut down the shrub growth on our own land. They said we had no right to build such a vocational workshop in their midst; we would ruin the community and destroy the value of their property. They were overruled by the Board of Zoning Appeals. None of the predicted disasters have occurred.

Over the years, property values around us in Albertson, and in the immediate neighborhood particularly, have soared astronomically. The value of additional land we would have liked to purchase when we first moved into Albertson, if we had had the funds, has quadrupled.

Everything we have constructed on this property has been landscaped with great concern and care that our center would blend into the environment and community around us. Yet when we built our Research and Training Center, in 1961, we faced the same hard core opposition, once again with warnings and challenges. By this time much of the vacant land surrounding us was being developed for private homes. Now we were expanding, they complained. Why didn't we stay with what we had? What right did we have to purchase additional land? Why should we be tax exempt?

So we went through it all again.

Albertson is a community now of upper middle class homes; most of its people are concerned with their own problems—they are frightened of what might happen to their homes, their environment, their jobs, frightened of all the uncertainties and changes of our times. In this they mirror similar communities and towns across Long Island and our country. Most of the people in Albertson still believe in us and our purpose, and most of them, I am convinced, are glad to have our beautiful campus in their midst. But to the organized group of active protesters, we became the enemy, the target of their pent-up antagonisms and fears.

They opposed us first in 1957 when we built the initial Abilities facility. They opposed us in 1961—and we won again. They opposed us for a third time, unsuccessfully, in 1965 when we decided to build a school for severely disabled children. They did not want us there; they did not want to look at severely disabled youngsters who finally had a chance, like other children, to go to school.

Our school became so successful that we had nearly two hundred students and a waiting list in some classes. To handle a student body of this size properly, it became obvious that we needed to expand our space in order to achieve the fullest possible education results.

In terms of the student population there will be no increase in numbers. Our mission is to be a pilot and experimental unit, to research in special education techniques, to train teachers, doctors, therapists, nurses, to write the special educational curriculum as it relates to the severely disabled child who has been homebound because of disability. The school, however, is not a residential home; the children have to be brought to school on school buses.

The new building that we planned to construct would help to relieve overcrowded conditions by providing a gymnasium and a cafeteria in addition to extra classroom space for learning laboratories and expanded curriculum development.

To house our intended population of 200 students from age three to high school graduates we needed the new facility. We did not and do not believe that it would serve our purpose as a research and teaching project to go beyond this number of students.

Nevertheless, the organized protesters were out in full cry against us with petitions, meetings and lawyers in the community; the quiet streets and homes became centers of conflict.

Once again the battle has been joined.

We are a minority, a sizable minority, we the handicapped. And because of that fact we have a kinship with all minorities, with black people and Jewish people, Puerto Ricans and Roman Catholics. We make common cause at least to the extent that all must struggle against prejudice and misunderstanding to achieve their rightful place and their rightful goals.

Albertson, Long Island, N.Y., is not a bad community, nor is it unique. It has all the aspects of peaceful suburban life, yet it also reflects the new patterns of our disturbed times—the fright and distrust and often unreasoning opposition to all minorities, to all change, to whatever is different, be it a day care center for children of the poor, a school for disturbed youngsters, a rehabitation center in a church, or anything that even remotely appears to threaten or challenge the sanctity of the suburban *status quo.* This is why Albertson is important.

This story of our struggle as handicapped workers, pupils, teachers and researchers is one fragment of what is happening to assorted minorities in countless other Albertson areas across this country today, in similar areas where seething turmoil, prejudice and often decisive open conflict has become part of the new suburban way of life.

This is why I believe our struggle to expand a school for crippled children has meaning and significance that reaches far beyond the tree-lined streets of one embattled Long Island community.

BUT NOT ON
OUR BLOCK

1

CONFLICT IN PARADISE

||||||||||||||||||||||||||||||||||||||||||||||||||||||||||||||||||||||||||||||||||||||||||||||

The conflict centered around the school and its students. And so it is important at the outset to understand what the school is, and who its students are—these young people who chatter and laugh and jostle one another in class, as children will, except that these youngsters do these things on crutches and in wheel chairs.

It would not be sufficient or wholly accurate to describe the Human Resources School, which we established at our Center in 1965, as merely a school for physically handicapped young people. What it is, in fact, is a school designed specifically for the most severely disabled children in the world, with classes that run from preschool through high school.

These children are not mentally retarded, emotionally disturbed, or brain damaged: these are children who in most cases never were able or allowed to go to school at all, who rarely, if ever, went outside their homes, who in many cases never even left the upstairs bedroom which was their whole world, their private prison. Their education rarely, if ever, amounted to much more than a homebound teacher who might come once or twice a week for an hour or two of instructions that were in most cases without direction or purpose because they were so limited educationally.

Because many of us at Human Resources experienced in our own childhood the inadequacies of homebound teaching, the lack of social contacts with our peers, the lack of the competitive drive of the classroom, we decided some years past that we could play a special role in the lives of the severely disabled children by establishing a school designed to meet the needs and problems of these forgotten youngsters who, despite severe physical disability, have all the same yearnings and dreams of any normal child. There were schools and centers for the deaf, the blind, the retarded, the emotionally disturbed child but not for a large group of disabled children who were not in these categories.

The world of these hidden homebound children was so little known, even by the authorities, that when we tried to get official sanction to start our school many would not believe that such children even existed, let alone the idea that such a school was possible; we had to go out and locate the children before they would believe us.

It took some time to do this because many parents kept the fact of their child's extreme disability a secret from the world. Sometimes they did this out of a sense of shame, more often out of fear of harm coming to their child, or because of the child's physical limitations. We did locate a number of these children, we talked to the dubious parents, we brought the parents —and the children—to our facilities where we had established the beginnings of our faculty.

This was our start—in an improvised classroom set up in our Human Resources Research Building. It was the beginning of the dramatic history of the first school of its kind in the world—a story of children coming out into the world, into the sunlight, of children learning to help each other and learning together. And of our learning to develop techniques for teaching in a field of education where at that time little or nothing of any serious character had been examined or tried. After all, many people used to think, why teach a child anything, if he has no place to go?

Yet there was, and there remains, a strong need for such education for children of this kind, children with rare illnesses for which there are no cures, children who in some instances may have only a few years of life. Do they not have a right to live whatever years they have left, few or many, to the fullest measure possible?

We obtained our charter when we were able to demonstrate the importance of and need for the school. Through the gifts of many wonderful people, we raised many thousands of dollars to build a specially created school house. We brought together a magnificent faculty and set up procedures where our children obtain regular education plus the special schooling these youngsters require. From our community we brought in many volunteers—including a number of

retired teachers—who helped tremendously in caring
for these children and their special needs. It would be
difficult if not impossible to operate the school without them.

One of our classrooms, for example, is a room to
teach our children to deal with problems of everyday
living—to teach a young lady how to make a bed or
cook a meal from a wheel chair, how to get into a
bathtub or out of it by herself, how to manage a home,
get her husband's breakfast or take care of her own
child.

Built with the full permission of local authorities,
despite the protesters, the school became a vital phase
of our whole operation. Within a few years its graduates were going into two- and four-year colleges.
Educators from all parts of the country and the world
came to see this activity and what it was doing and
how.

The success of the school, the increasing numbers of
students crowding in, the demands for admission all
combined to create a new situation. We needed more
classroom space, even to serve the nearly two hundred
student enrollment reached by 1969. We needed, in
addition, areas for relaxation, for extracurricular programs in music and drama; we needed a full-scale lecture hall for major assemblies, commencement and
graduations. The combined gym and cafeteria in the
new building would give us this capacity.

It had taken some time to learn what we needed in
various fields—what kind of gymnasium and physical
education program would serve youngsters like ours,

for example. We knew now; we had spent five years in learning the special equipment indicated for our gymnasium. We knew also that we needed a cafeteria designed especially for our own youngsters and teachers, our volunteer teachers' aides, our research and training faculty. Because of crowded conditions as we grew, we found that our children and these volunteers had to study together in cloak rooms and research laboratories and even hallways.

So we decided to build an addition to our school to house these needed facilities which were not included in the original building. It would be two stories high but it would have sufficient steel and foundation so that one day, if desired and needed, we might add three stories. It would be a carefully designed school building in every respect. The entire area would be landscaped. In fact, our existing buildings were in the form of an "L." The new building would nestle inside the "L" and would be shielded from the street by the existing structures.

All of this was in the process of planning and developing in 1969. I went out once again to raise funds for this undertaking. We were able to obtain most of these funds totaling more than $3,000,000 from individuals, American industry and from major American foundations who understood and believed in and wanted to support what we were doing.

It was about this same time that a new zoning concept, known as Educational-Cultural Zoning, had been developed in a nearby Long Island community. It provided that any church, synagogue, educational or charitable institution could build a building beyond the normal height allowed, or even of larger dimensions, but with a height limit, if its purpose, design and usage were deemed by the town authorities to be of cultural or educational advantage to the community. Once this zoning was adopted by the town, any application which conformed to its provisions would be granted. The interminable protests that came with every application for a variance would be ended. The ordinance would bring sense out of chaos.

Under the leadership of Supervisor Robert Meade, North Hempstead began to develop a similar educational-cultural zoning code with a height restriction of seventy-five feet. Town officials and architects came to us and to other interested groups in the area and sought our opinion. We decided it was a wonderful idea. It had been successful in nearby Hempstead; it would be equally successful, we felt sure, in North Hempstead. Indeed, with our new building, and our future possible needs in mind we decided to be the first to apply for a building permit under the new ordinance.

We and our attorneys decided to appear before the town board to urge passage of the new ordinance and to seek authorization under this educational-cultural zoning provision so that we could begin construction of the new school.

It was then that the opposition forces in Albertson moved in. This time apparently they felt they had a real cause, a real base for their attack. For the first time they could start mounting a major offensive against us in the community, one that could draw in many who had not participated before. The line of attack was clear and basic: *Viscardi wants to build a five-story building. Do you want that kind of thing here? It's going to be worse than a slum. Is that what you want in your community? A five-story factory ? . . .*

What resulted in the winter of 1970 at the first hearing was something I never personally experienced before and hope never to experience again. To me the voice of a mob is not only indecent, it is uncivilized. In one mob scene I see all the mobs that ever stormed out against justice and tried to take over the destiny of people.

It was a mob that turned out at that first hearing before the North Hempstead Town Board, a mob that fought against both the proposed new ordinance and our petition for the school addition under its provisions.

The opposition had come in force, jamming the hearing room and the corridors and the stairways, spurred on by the leaders and their door-to-door campaign against us. They were there to cry us down—with or without the chairman's recognition.

They numbered several hundred and all were trying to edge their way into the standing-room-only hearing in the North Hempstead town hall. They were residents, homeowners, voters. There to support us were some of the parents of the disabled children in our school, as well as some friendly neighbors. A number had their children with them.

Mostly, however, they were representative of a

cross-section of upper middleclass suburban America, roused now into a noisy, determined, angry throng jamming into the hall.

And the target of their outrage, directly and inevitably, was me since I represented the facility they so violently opposed.

The meeting itself was a seething thing. Spectators, chattering among themselves, talked to each other as our witnesses tried to testify. Half-said, half-heard words were whispered loudly, side remarks calculated to disturb the hearing: *This is just a ploy he's pulling; they want to turn the whole place into a factory to make money. . . . How much of it is he going to use for those crippled kids and how much is he going to use for the plant? How much are they costing us in lost taxes. ? . . .*

Many of these people did not understand that Abilities is not a profit-making operation but a workshop and training facility founded on the principle that the disabled who were trained there would do so on terms by which they would support themselves out of their earnings. Because of its educational purposes, Abilities was tax exempt from the start. This was essential in order to support the severe disabilities of the personnel. Beyond that exemption, these workers accepted no grants, no assistance. All the rest—buildings, land, equipment and salaries, was paid for out of earnings for work performed, while the workers supported themselves instead of being supported.

There had been good years and bad. In some there were dollars left over after all wages and bills were paid. These dollars were put aside for years when there was no surplus, only losses. There were more bad years than good but overall we managed to survive.

Abilities had been able to put aside enough to carry it through the bad economic days that came at the close of the 1960's. Things were bad everywhere at that time. People were out of work and jobs scarce. We had laid off more than half of our staff, we were drawing on our reserves and struggling to hold on and to change direction in order to provide more work at the time this fight came upon us.

These thoughts crowded in upon me as I waited to be heard, as the words, the interruptions by the protesters sputtered and swirled in the air in that angry, noisy gathering of people shouting against whatever disagreed with their view, applauding their spokesmen wildly, breaking into statements by our people again and again, so that the chairman had to rap for order.

Amid intermittent bursts of applause, one opposition spokesman declared: ". . . After the presentation this morning, I must state that we are not against Human Resources. We are not the 'black cowboys in black hats.' . . . I personally could not wish Mr. Viscardi or Human Resources any greater luck in the undertakings that he is presently at. It is ridiculous to think that anybody in this room could be against any of the work that is being done. Let us get into the specific reasons why we are against this specific application. . . ."

But then came the reasons. Apparently it did not

matter to them that architecturally the plan was beautiful or that our proposals had involved months of careful development to make sure that they would enhance the whole community. All of this was simply brushed aside as being without relevance.

Still they insisted publicly that they really loved Abilities. It was only this additional construction they opposed. We had heard it all before, from their earliest efforts to keep us from turning the first shovelful of earth in the construction of our first building. Each step was a battle against shifting legal arguments. No one ever said in any petition that what they really didn't like was to look at us, our people, our school and its crippled children.

One of our mothers, whose lovely but severely handicapped daughter was one of our school's brightest stars, related an incident that happened to her during a visit at the home of one of our neighbors. The neighbor, who did not realize her visitor was the mother of one of our students, began denouncing Human Resources School as well as other activities on our campus. The mother tried to explain some of the school's good points, but the neighbor broke in with, "How would you like to spend thousands of dollars for your home, and then walk out on your back porch and see a group of handicapped people? How would you like to see that?"

This was what really disturbed her. This was the deeply ingrained truth that they rarely dare put into words.

"What about the grounds, don't you think they are

beautiful?" the mother of the handicapped girl countered. "Doesn't it do your heart good to see those children playing, laughing, happy? They have their own picnic groups, and playgrounds. They play ball. Don't you feel anything for them? Doesn't it make you feel any better to know that here they can laugh and be happy?"

"It isn't a pleasant sight," the neighbor insisted.

"How would you feel if you had a handicapped child of your own?" the mother asked gently. The woman said nothing. The mother went on, "You would feel differently in that case. I know. I have a child who's been handicapped from birth. She is very beautiful. We love her very much."

As the mother explained it to me, "When I told her that, she just stopped short. That was the end of our conversation. She turned and walked away."

Protests against our school, our children, our purposes, were not isolated episodes on Long Island. They were a pattern. Scenes of anger, insults and shouting have become familiar. The eager young lawyer doing battle is also a part of the pattern.

What do they protest against or object to? Projects Long Island communities have rejected because of organized objections include nurseries, libraries, low-cost housing for the poor and the aged, youth centers, day care centers.

Meetings before boards and commissions last long into the night as the organized neighborhood cadres descend upon the officials to voice their objections, and the attorneys pound home their carefully prepared statements. Many of these protests appear to the outsider to be wholly without rational basis. They represent a new nation-wide form of what one attorney called "middle-aged activism blended with five o'clock martinis."

There are many reasons for their protests and their fears. Sometimes the fears have basic justification; a new jet airport in the center of a suburban area, for example, could badly damage a community. Wisdom and understanding and satisfactory efforts to find solutions can solve many problems when they are problems. But too often the objections raised are simply a generalized counterattack against progress, or based upon superstition, ignorance and fear.

One local news story provided a clue to underlying reasons for these patterns of protest. It quoted the head of the Department of Social Relations of John Hopkins University, Professor Peter Rossi, who said, "It's a fear that the status quo, which seems to be working so well, will be destroyed. . . ."

What they really fear includes intangibles beyond the physical environment. For some, at least, it includes the fear of even looking at a crippled child, at a man or woman, young or old, who may have lost a limb or who were, as I was, born with twisted stumps for legs. They recoil from such sights in a kind of primitive horror at whatever differs from the norm.

They have fled the city to get away from its problems—dope, dirt, taxes, crime, poor schools, black people—only to find the same problems. Many live in fear that their next door neighbors in the suburbs may change color, that they may look out to see their little white girl playing with a little black boy on the side-walk beyond their neatly-clipped hedges.

Not all of suburbia is bound by these deep-rooted terrors, not even a majority. But it is there, a pervading reality. It is there, it is vocal and usually well-organized. The noise and the shouting provide some of these people with an identity, an outlet for frustration, for the army of uncertainties with which they live in their heavily-mortgaged fortress.

To what extent could I hope to change these attitudes? How much is any militant opposition amenable to reason? Could I go into the homes of the people who have challenged us so often and talk them out of their protests?

I might make some change in their attitude toward disabled people but it would be a change in degree, not in kind. And that is the central issue. I could make them understand that disabled people can work, can be educated, trained, can learn to support themselves, can become the same, not different from others. But could I change anyone's prejudice against having me as a son-in-law, me with my two stumps incased in artificial limbs? Could I change people's prejudice against having a school full of crippled children in their neighborhood?

The answer is no. The answer is that they could believe in all the other things, all the brotherhood, all the nonsegregation for whatever minority may be in-volved—as long as it is somewhere else, not in their community. This is the problem; it has been the problem down all the years.

Are the problems we encounter in the new suburbs really different from what I faced as a crippled boy fighting my way on the streets of the West Side of New York? Is it any different from the problems I faced as a young man filled with ideals and the concepts of chivalry and honor, trying to get a job, struggling around on twisted stumps before I had artificial limbs? Is it any different from my problems in adolescence, and later after I had my limbs, when I hoped to find someone I could love and who would love me, someone with whom I could spend the rest of my life? I don't think so. I found such a person in those days and I am one of the fortunate ones who found happiness with a wonderful wife and four wonderful daughters. But there were others who did not. I did help to change some minds, some attitudes. But again it was only in degree, not in the flint-hard realities, not at the North Hempstead town board hearing with its cries of anger.

Life sometimes seems almost deliberately to pit one challenge against another. Just prior to the time of this bitter winter hearing, when the whole destiny and future of our school and of Human Resources itself in some measure was at stake, I received a word from Republican leaders in our community that they wanted me to run for Congress.

I was assured that I would have the strongest kind of support, that I would not be merely another freshman congressman but would be able to play a role for the cause of handicapped people on a much wider stage.

I cannot deny that I found the offer appealing and exciting. It was not the kind of proposal anyone could reject lightly. Yet this sudden and unexpected offer of a possible chance to serve in a new role came at a moment when I faced an even more immediate challenge closer to home. How could I leave my people at that moment, for whatever cause?

The impending struggle lay just ahead; the battle lines were drawn. My whole life had been dedicated to this cause. How could I accept a new role at this critical moment—or try, if elected, to carry on two roles, one in Albertson, one in Washington?

At that moment I faced one of the most important decisions of my life. These were my people, this was my cause. We had become the symbol, in that explosive moment, we were the target of the new hate, the new prejudice.

We the disabled had become the enemy for some of our neighbors in Albertson.

2

PICKET FENCES AND BOLTED DOORS

Who were these individuals, these neighbors, to whom we had become a foe to be contained, even driven out? Why had we, our particular minority of disabled workers and students, become such a primary target in their minds?

To understand the answer to this, one must understand also the character and problems that shape this world of picket fences and well-locked doors. The answer lies in the individuals and families migrating into America's new suburban community to escape the blight of the cities. The new suburbs become the last line of defense. Here they must stand against whatever seems to present even a potential threat, against any minority seeking a foothold, crippled or black or Puerto Rican, against any possible challenge to their new-found status quo. Nothing must be allowed to approach even remotely the urban decay from which they have run.

They fled because they were frightened of the cities and the barrios. They fled from muggings and murders, tensions and riots to the new utopian communi-

ties beyond the cities—to Long Island or Wellesley
Hills or Piedmont, to a thousand suburban developments.

And in these new housing developments to which
they moved—often at inflated prices combined with
crushing mortgages—they found much of what they
sought, as well as other things they had not considered. They found green grass, open skies, playing
fields for their youngsters; they were now away from
the noise and endless harrassment of the city, away
from polluted air and smog.

They also found that many of the problems they had
sought to escape in the city were following them into
the suburbs. Black people and other minority groups
were also moving from the cities to the peace and quiet
of the suburbs. Except that the minority people were
finding it difficult to buy or rent homes and many
were forced to take inadequate housing in what
amounted to newly emerging suburban slums. Other
groups also were pressing; other problems and tensions of the urban world had moved out into the suburbs, too.

A new turmoil was beginning to develop in this
suburban situation. And out of this a new protective
enclave philosophy began to take shape in many of
these heavily-mortgaged upper middle-class neighborhoods. Any challenge, any intrusion, any low-cost
housing for low-income people had to be fought.

Despite mortgages, amortization, auto loans, commuting fares and all the rest of the overwhelming load
many of these people carry, the house on utopia court

was still their private preserve, their picket-fence fortress.

Here they would stand their ground against all comers.

Behind the attitudes of the new suburbias are factors and forces which few in these neighborhoods openly discuss. Few admit even to themselves, much less openly, what they really feel and mean in these matters.

Fear, for example, is one of these forces. Fear grows in such developments; each individual family and home, finding itself facing real or imaginary threats in the new paradise, is ready to take action against its enemies, often spurred on by a leadership that whips up the neighborhood to a degree totally out of proportion to the problem itself—if there is any actual problem at all.

You have to try to understand their fears, their frustrations. Once moved into their new utopia, they find the tax bills are just as high or higher than in the city; they find that their costs in many things are doubled, that transportation, land taxes and school taxes have soared out of reason and reach. The fortress world they create must be held like a battle line. Their high-priced dwellings sit like pillboxes, ready to fend off any interloper.

They fear newcomers, other peoples, other races, other colors, people of other backgrounds, cultures, religions. They fear welfare costs. They fear they will be paying taxes to support a deterioration if any change is allowed. They refuse to vote for their own school budget and so the school district has to go on an austerity budget or resubmit an amended budget for approval.

Fear shapes many of the concepts, many of the actions—fear and prejudice. Prejudice is equally important but no one talks about it, certainly not openly. No one comes and declares that he is against Blacks or Jews or the Irish or Italians as such. Other reasons are always put forward but everybody understands. Low-cost housing is opposed solely for economic reasons—not because the people who moved in might be the wrong color.

Prejudice lies at the core of an overwhelming percent of all such protests, against the handicapped as against the others. Prejudice is not a single thing, it is a compendium that includes fear, superstition, misinformation and ignorance. The handicapped know prejudice and feel its sting as does any black person.

I remember familiar patterns out of my own boyhood. As a child with grotesque, thick-soled boots on my stumps, I learned to face and deal with my juvenile peers, on New York's gang-ridden streets, to fight when I had to, to live with the taunting cries of "Ape Man" and "Monster."

Their outcries against me, their physical attacks were not because I had harmed them but because I was different, because I had stumps instead of legs, because I was a freak who perhaps, in the minds of some people, should never have been born.

All his life the handicapped person has to deal with

such attitudes. They are always easy to recognize, in a glance or word, a tone of voice, perhaps in the pity of adult eyes looking down upon a half-made creature.

You learn to live with prejudice, to understand its subtle nuances and subterfuges and disguises.

Many people sincerely believe they love the handicapped—so much so that they won't come to visit Abilities and our school "because," as they put it, "it makes me so terribly sad." But the real reason is usually a familiar one: subconscious fear, fear that it might happen to them or to someone in their family, to their own little girl who lives right across the street from our school, from our children who walk on crutches or ride in wheel chairs or on litters.

There must always be someone to blame, someone to become the target. The community that does not vote its local school a budget, because its people do not want to pay the extra taxes to cover that budget, tries to make us responsible. So they say, "In 1968–69, Abilities, you had four million dollars worth of sales. Why aren't you paying taxes to help us with our tax burden?" Of course, they didn't look at the other years, 1967 and 1966 and 1965, or 1970 when we lost more than a million dollars. Nor do they examine how much we really earned on that amount of sales, after all expenses were paid. So we have a school for severely handicapped children which receives state support for part of its operations and the rest of the funds in the form of contributions that come from many sources. Since there is such a high burden of medical cost to these families, no tuition is charged to

our students who have no other school they can attend. But the neighbors worry that while we run our
private school we are not also paying to run their
public school.

And what happens is that these fears and misunderstandings build to where people find a reason for their
superstition, a justification for their prejudice, an excuse for their ignorance. And one excuse is often as
good as another.

I suppose everyone is entitled to his own prejudice
so long as it does no harm. But people are not entitled
to let their prejudice lash out at others, or at the rights
of other human beings. They are not entitled to mob
action, they are not entitled to discourtesy. I am not
asking them to love us or support us. But I do not
expect them to try to drive us away because they do
not like to look at a child with a twisted body.

Minority status is a special thing; each group must
search its own needs, fight its own battles; and although the situations often overlap, the problems are
often closely identified. The minority called the disabled has been oppressed for centuries. In ancient days,
the Spartans would take malformed infants and throw
them over the cliff. Other peoples have done the same
in later centuries. Some still do, in a thousand different ways.

Suburbia of the Seventies has its counterparts in
other places, other times. If you study the cultures of
the past, or go into Asia, or Western Europe, you find
compassion for the disabled, you find a willingness to
do something for them. But where most fall apart is

in the area of giving them equality of opportunity to support themselves. Too few among us are concerned enough to change anything for the benefit of the disabled, too few take the trouble ever to remember, for example, that there's no way in the world for a man in a wheel chair to enter certain public buildings, churches or schools or to go down the aisle of an airliner or a train—if the aisle is too narrow for a wheel chair or is inaccessable by ramp or elevator.

Some cultures, otherwise considered modern, still cling to virtually barbaric customs and ideas regarding this and other minorities. The truth is that in many cities of the western world with their antiquated structures, even in the heart of modern cities such as Rome and Paris, the disabled individual has great difficulty because of the architectural barriers in buildings and houses. This is also true of the aged, or persons with accident injuries or women in advanced stages of pregnancy. There are some groups and individuals who are beginning to become concerned and whom we have been able to interest in this problem. Many of these have been executives of American corporations.

In Asia, where I was invited to lecture about our own activities in America, I ran into the concept that some Japanese still consider disability as a reflection of sin or guilt on the part of the family to which the disabled person belongs. Members of the family support and care for this disabled person as a part of their atonement or *karma*.

Since the war in Korea, wheel chairs and crutches

are a familiar sight in that country. This is true both
among the poorer people and those in institutions. At
the same time, examples of bearers who carry their
disabled masters on their shoulders from place to
place occur in many cases involving severely disabled
former officers of the Korean army. At the time of my
visit which was some years ago, I was told that this
was done because of the rough streets and roads and
also because human labor in Korea is so inexpensive.

These human bearers were drawn from the home-
less men who sleep under the bridges along the river
in Seoul, Korea. They are hired virtually as beasts of
burden. With the traditional A-frame which was so
popular for carrying ammunition during the Korean
War, the bearers trot all over Seoul carrying all sorts
of things, even large pieces of furniture. Why not
carry a man as well—if he has the price? I doubt if
Asians see any significance in these human bearers
carrying disabled Korean veterans. It is a part of their
way of life.

I cite these varying attitudes and approaches toward
the disabled in Europe and Asia as an indication of the
wide diversity in concepts, as well as misconceptions
and outmoded thinking about the disabled. Ignorance
and misunderstanding are neither new nor localized.
The attitudes and objections to us by some of our
neighbors are simply additional examples of such
misunderstanding.

They say we are a business, a factory. They say we
ought to pay taxes—forgetting that Abilities is an educational center, a workshop, a training facility, a pilot

project, non-profit, and tax exempt.

There have been times, of course, when I have been outraged at the episodes in this long, seemingly endless struggle, times when I have walked away from these sessions with a sense of despair, of helplessness and hopelessness that we as a people could survive our misunderstandings, our internecine struggles, our failures to learn to live together not as majorities or minorities but as human beings. We had no idea then how hard this struggle was to become in the months ahead.

Yet, in a curious way, we had always felt it would be a great victory if we had to close down because there was no further need for the Human Resources Center. If there were jobs available in industry and commerce for the severely disabled, and if we knew where to locate such positions for our people, Abilities could and should close its doors. If there were places in regular schools for the severely disabled students in Human Resources School, then this school should close its doors.

More knowledge and understanding, and new specially-designed physical plants are needed before this can be achieved. It may never be entirely possible. But with each individual worker or student who goes forth, who leaves us for a regular job or school or college, a victory is won. Another disabled person becomes the same, not different from the rest of the world.

This would be the real victory.

3

PERSONAL AND URGENT:
FOR THE MAJORITY

||||||||||||||||||||||||||||||||||||||||||||||||||||||||||||||||||||||||||||||||||||||||||||||||||||||||||||||||||||||

By a twist of coincidence in the closing weeks of
1969 two seemingly opposed aspects of my life and
career converged on what appeared to be a collision
course.

One of these aspects was the growing challenge
from the protesters, now fully organized, with an active and aggressive lawyer who it was reported was
determined to go to any legal lengths necessary to win
this case.

The other was totally different—the political situation into which I had been thrown through no volition
of my own but because local Republican leaders believed I could serve the country best if I agreed to run
for the House of Representatives. It was a high honor
to be asked to serve in such a role. It involved deep
commitments.

Pressures seemed to come from all sides, from Albany and Washington, from industrialists and businessmen who were my personal friends and associates. This crescendo of pressure mounted in intensity
in these weeks. Despite my openly-avowed determina-

tion not to accept the offer, in view of the critical situation at Human Resources, it was clear that some important people were making an all-out effort to change my mind.

But I had made my cause that of disabled people. I was not about to run out on that. I was willing to fight for this cause, here on the scene. If I considered it necessary and advisable I would be perfectly willing, if all else failed, to lead a peaceful and entirely legal march—in wheel chairs—to the North Hempstead Town Hall and hold a prayer session on the Town Hall steps with friends and neighbors and all our disabled men and women and children taking part.

Because I was locked into this struggle, perspectives were difficult to keep in line, particularly in regard to the new political forces that had been injected into my already over-complicated life. I was told by the political leaders that I was respected and loved—they said because of what we had achieved. But this assault in which I found myself pilloried by some of the neighbors made me wonder if the description still applied.

Nevertheless, the suggestion that I run for national office was not without attractive aspects. It was a high honor to be asked to run for Congress. And it offered a whole new role—an important and exciting new role. I cannot deny that I was tempted by this possibility.

This had come first in the form of a simple phone call from the state capitol building in Albany.

It was a day in the early winter, as Christmas decorations and wreaths began to appear and candles began to light windows in Albertson, when I received a phone call from State Senator, John Caemmerer, who happened also to be the political leader of our district.

I had met Senator Caemmerer on several occasions; I knew him as one of the most respected leaders of the community and of the state government in Albany. I did not know that he was calling after a conference with Republican leaders meeting in Albany with Governor Nelson A. Rockefeller.

The Senator informed me that he had had discussions concerning the possibility of my agreeing to run for the House of Representatives in Washington. He had talked it over with the Governor as well as with other leaders of the Republican Party in New York.

"They are all very excited about the idea that you might run," he told me. "They think it would be a wonderful move from every point of view."

It would be difficult in such a situation not to be flattered. The top leaders of the Republican party, meeting with the Governor of New York, were asking me to be a candidate for Congress.

I told him how honored I was by this suggestion, and this phone call. The Congress of the United States is the heart of this Republic, the heart of our freedom; it is the duly elected will of the people. I told the Senator that I did not know what to say, that I needed time to think this over, I just couldn't say yes or no over the telephone. Senator Caemmerer said, "That's reasonable. But at least—can I tell the Governor that you're interested?"

I told him of course that I was interested. "I don't

think there's a man alive who wouldn't be interested in serving in the Congress of the United States."

There was a long pause, as if he were waiting for me to drop the other political shoe—by saying yes, I would run. After a moment, I said, "Senator, give me a little time to consider this, to talk it over with some of my close friends. Then I can let you know. Would you mind if I took until after Christmas?"

"That seems fair enough," he said. "It's only a couple of weeks away. Meanwhile, when I get down to New York I'd like to come to see you, and we can talk some more about it. I can tell you some reasons why you ought to do this, and help you with your decision."

We agreed that I would think about it. I would let him know.

Almost immediately following that call things began to happen. I not only had to explore the concept in my own mind, I had to discuss it with others, with associates at Human Resources, with Lucile, with certain friends. And this really was no time of year to explore such matters—so close to Christmas, to children returning for vacation from school and college, to family gatherings, to all that goes with the Christmas season.

Nevertheless, as my first action, I called a meeting of the Executive Board of Human Resources Center and invited a select group of its close friends. Meeting in a private dining room of the CIT Corporation in New York, the group included C.W. Dow, vice-president of this important financial firm, and a distinguished gathering of American business leaders, including presidents and other officials of a number of corporations.

None knew in advance the subject of the meeting; I wanted it that way for a reason. These were my friends as well as my associates in Human Resources Center. I wanted their unpremeditated, spontaneous, instinctive reaction. I apologized for the shortness of time. "What I want really is your own ideas on a subject of importance concerning possible new responsibilities I may assume. You're aware of other responsibilities I have already. I don't say I'll accept your recommendations. The final decision has to be made by me in my own conscience."

I told them of the Senator's calling to suggest that I run for Congress. I said I would have the full support of the Governor and state party leaders. I said that they believed I would also have wide bipartisan support. They were convinced I could and would be elected.

I explained my own feeling concerning the role of Congress, the honor for me personally if I were elected, and even more importantly the responsibilities assumed by any individual who accepts such a role.

We reviewed together some of the most immediate considerations. The three basic divisions of our operation of Human Resources Center in Albertson were Abilities, the Human Resources School and the Human Resources Research and Training Center. Each had a competent and effective executive leader, each was a reasonably autonomous unit. If I decided to leave these activities, I would be able to do so with reasonable certainty of a continuity of effective top management. These were young men, all disabled, who had developed primarily under my leadership. Were they ready for full-command responsibility until another chief executive could be found to fill my post?

There were, I pointed out, other questions. Do I want to leave? Was I attracted by the prospect of being a congressman? Could I, as Senator Caemmerer put it, serve the cause of the disabled better as a member of Congress than I could sitting in Albertson? Would I be just another freshman congressman or even more than before a spokesman for our cause? Was this, as the Senator urged, something I owed to the cause I serve?

"I am certain the Senator meant what he said," I told them. "I am not so sure about the evaluation itself. It might very well be a disservice to the disabled. I want to know frankly your feelings about this whole suggestion."

Around the table, for a moment, no one spoke. I waited. E.U. DaParma, chairman of our Human Resources Board, broke that sudden hush. An outstanding business leader, former president of the Sperry Rand Office Systems Division, he is one of my long-time friends. He is also perfectly willing at all times to state his views bluntly. In this instance, however, he said that he had mixed feelings about the issue. He did not want to urge me either way. "Personally I think you should run," he said. "But in another way I'm reluctant to recommend that you do."

The next speaker took a strikingly different tack. Bernie Fixler, a member of our board and head of his own industrial company on Long Island, was emphatically and totally opposed. "Worst thing in the world you could do, Hank," he declared. "Do you realize the ugliness of political life, the treachery, the dishonesty that goes on? Do you realize the people you'd have to consort with, who would put pressure on you? How could you possibly think of subordinating the noble things that are part of your work and life to become involved in a world that is cruel, that is dishonest?"

Bernie was a staunch Democrat and generally opposed to what Republicans in political office stood for. But I knew that this in no way colored his views, even subconsciously. Bernie's opposition here was wholly non-partisan. There was no such implication whatever. It was wrong for me, he said, to give up what I was doing for the mess in Washington, Republican or Democratic. Others around the table felt the same way. CIT vice-president Dow put it like this, "Well, if you were working for CIT and you came to our corporate administration, of which I, as a financial vice-president, am a member, you'd find that you'd have to make up your mind whether you wanted to work for CIT or become a congressman. You couldn't do both. If you chose being a congressman, you'd be through with us." For an instant he paused, facing me across the table, his expression gravely concerned.

"Do you intend, Hank, to give up your job of running Human Resources Center?"

I agreed that I couldn't do both jobs full time. The best I could do would be a division of time—shuttling back and forth on the plane, Monday to Thursday there, Thursday to Monday here.

"No," Dow said, "You'd have to decide. I think you'd be foolish to give up Human Resources Center and the things for which we need you. But under no circumstances could I condone your continued activity in the Center if you make the decision to run for Congress."

This was their opinion, as businessmen, Republican and Democratic, in a number of fields. One fact loomed clearly: Except DaParma who was torn by his own leanings, as I myself was, every one of these men was opposed.

I thanked them all for their time and concern, as well as their frankness. I said I would let them know when I reached my decision. They knew how difficult this would be for me. My wife Lucile was involved, my family, my own personal life. And those things for which I had worked—the new building, our people, the school. I had also to decide whether or not I had built the team strong enough that I could turn from it, full time or part time.

As our meeting broke up, I told them, "There is a very real temptation to accept. The challenge of a second career, of perhaps being able to play a part in national issues that affect the disabled as well as the nation, is strong. I would be dishonest not to say that

I am tempted strongly, for many reasons."

So finished my luncheon meeting with the members of our board.

It was after that meeting that I realized the depth of personal conflict in which I was involved. And as always, it was not I alone who was involved, or my family, or my own desires. It was also the basic issue, this minority of which I was and must be throughout my life, a part. The whole meaning of minority shapes itself in the fact of permanence. You may run, hide, ignore it, fight it. But it remains. And you remain part of it, if you will or not.

In the days that followed I spent many hours examining where this could lead. As it began to crystallize in my thoughts, the issue revolved around a key question: Where could I achieve the most, not merely for myself or the cause of disability, but forgetting my own situation, and trying to see the thing in clear perspective. Was my role to serve this cause, or to find a wider horizon? Or was there any wider horizon to search for than a handful of humanity that happened to be called the crippled and blind?

In the midst of my own concern with this problem —as the Christmas lights and trees and wreaths and ribbons whirled around us at home and at Human Resources and throughout the community, I began to be aware of other pressures. Not heavy, or threatening, not in the least unfriendly. But pressure still. I received phone calls from my friends, urging me to accept. There were other more significantly political calls also. One was from a long-time friend, Leonard

Hall, who had been Eisenhower's campaign manager, and who was Nixon's campaign manager when Nixon lost by inches to John Kennedy. Hall had been also chairman of the Republican party—a venerable and able lawyer, a loyal friend who lives in Oyster Bay. "I was in Washington last night," Hall said, "and I went over, of course, to visit the White House, and later dropped in on Republican Headquarters. I'm delighted to hear that you're a fair-haired candidate for Congress. Hank, I hope you're going to run. Both the White House and National Headquarters have asked me to put pressure on you to do this."

I said, "Len, I appreciate your calling me."

"Just remember," Len said, "you wouldn't be just another freshman congressman. You'd be a national figure immediately. You'd be on every front page. You could do a lot more for your cause."

I said, "Len, I've heard all the arguments, and I have to think about it."

"Well, think about it, sure," he said. "But why not give me a chance to talk to you and twist your arm? I'm your friend and I want you to do it."

But Len's tone was gentle, and we said we would talk again.

Not long after that, I had a call from William Casey, one of the most influential, affluent tax lawyers in America and now chairman of the S. E. C. He was a classmate of mine at Fordham University and also a close personal friend of President Nixon. "I'm just back from seeing the President," Bill said. "We and some of the top people in the administration want you to run for Congress. And I hope you won't be foolish enough to say no. This is very significant; you must accept it, Hank. You must."

"Bill, I appreciate deeply what you are saying."

He indicated to me again that there were a number of persons in high office who would be pleased if I were to accept. He did not amplify this statement and I did not press for further details.

I was aware of the importance of Bill's phone call, knowing that he was close to the White House. I thanked him for his call. It was a moment I could not forget. Nevertheless, I had to tell Bill as I had told Len Hall, "I want to think it out, Bill. But I will let you know."

Perhaps, I felt, I had not made it clear to them that I was torn by divided loyalties, and goals. The story of America has always held tremendous meaning in my mind. Perhaps it is because I am a son of immigrant Italian parents, brought up by a wonderful, old-fashioned, story-book Italian mother, reared under all the problems of my own physical deformities and yet able to find a way through to opportunities. Our history to me has always been a moving, dramatic pageant. If not always perfect, neither was it always wrong. It is a story marked by moments of incomparable valor, not only on the battlefield but equally in the halls of government. I think of early leaders who boldly affixed their signatures to a Declaration that, had it failed, would have cost their lives. It was in these terms of struggle and courage that I saw the issue, the meaning of our Congress today.

At the same time there was the other meaning, the needs of these special human beings with whom and for whom I worked.

Yet even as the tensions rose regarding forthcoming hearings before the Town Board regarding the school, the protests, the possible findings of the board, and even as pressures increased on me to at least consider possible wider horizons of service at a national political level, the daily demands and needs and immediacy of my role at Human Resources Center continued at increasing tempo.

It was a round of the dramatic, the challenging, the unexpected. It was lectures and speeches at conventions or on university campuses. It was a foreign embassy calling to seek information on how to start an Abilities in their country; it was an official in the government in Washington calling for advice about a new process in physical rehabilitation for handicapped adolescents.

Or it was a call in the middle of the night from a city nearly two hundred miles distant—a distraught call from a mother whose severely disabled son had been thrown into jail that night on a drunken driving charge that could wreck his career and his life.

4

SEIZE AND ARREST:
A MINORITY REPORT

||||||||||||||||||||||||||||||||||||||||||||||||||||||||||||||||||||||||||||||||||||||||||||||||||

It was long past twelve that night when I was aroused from sleep by the telephone's ringing. The caller was a woman in a state of hysteria and it was several moments before I could calm her down and begin to get some idea of what this was all about.

At the onset of this experience all I could gather was that her son, paralyzed from an early injury and confined to a wheel chair, had been arrested and that she did not know exactly where they had taken him or what was about to happen to him.

I knew this mother through my own early friendship with her husband Carl, when he and I were working in the rehabilitation field in Washington, D.C., during World War II. I had been with the Red Cross; most of my work at that time was with returning Army and Air Force disabled at Walter Reed Hospital. Carl and I developed a close friendship; I had visited him and his wife at their home on several occasions.

Carl had died several years before this post-midnight telephone call. They had only one child—this

paralyzed son who, despite his handicap, had done
well in school and college and who now, in his mid-
twenties, was holding down an executive position in
a merchandising concern in his home town, was engaged to be married and was on his way to a trium-
phant career when this unlooked-for episode occurred.

The details, as the mother outlined them over the
phone, were sparse. Her son had been in some kind of
accident in the car, she told me. No one apparently
had been hurt, little if any damage was done to the car
or himself or anyone else. "All I know," she told me,
"is that he's been arrested because he was drunk. The
police called and said he'd been in an accident. I can't
understand it. My son doesn't drink. Sometimes he'll
have a glass of sherry or a cocktail. It simply isn't
something he does."

The real problem, of course, was what was happening to him at that moment. Handling a severely disabled person requires understanding and care. Great
harm and injury can result from improper treatment.
Where would they put him? How would they get him
in and out of his chair? Where would they keep him
while he was in custody?

I reminded the mother that I had lectured in their
town a few months earlier and had telephoned her on
that occasion. At the luncheon where I spoke I had sat
next to a judge who was concerned with problems of
the handicapped and with whom I had since had some
warm and friendly correspondence. I promised the
mother I would get in touch with him first thing in the

morning. He could tell us where we stood, and give us the name of a good lawyer.

Over the phone I could hear the mother's sobbing. I realized how helpless she was in a situation of this kind. Carl would have handled it somehow if he were there. But Carl was dead and she was alone.

I realized also that because I was his friend and hers, because I had met the boy in earlier years and his parents and I had talked about his condition and where he could best go to school and college—because of all this, I had a special obligation at that particular moment to this mother and her son, whatever the facts proved to be.

It was then about three-thirty or a quarter to four in the morning. I said I would leave as soon as I could get dressed and ready. The drive would take four or five hours. I would call my jurist friend as soon as I reached town in the morning. Through him I was sure we could obtain a reliable attorney for this case.

Throughout that long, lonely drive across the darkness and the dawn, I found myself concerned as to what I could do in the matter. I had met this young man only on a few occasions but everything I knew about him was good. He was anything but the playboy type, the hard drinker. I knew he was engaged; I recall that we had received an announcement some weeks before.

I reached the city around eight, called the judge and visited him at his home. We called the mother but she had had no further word from her son—she explained that her son told her the police allowed him only one

phone call. The judge put us in touch with a young
attorney familiar with the local routines; the lawyer
and I met at his office half an hour later.

I asked him if he'd been able to get any line on what
had happened to young Carl.

"Yes—I've located him through the police," the attorney said. "He's charged with drunken driving. I
want to get over there right away to stop it. Let's go."

On the way over the lawyer explained that they
were not holding the trial in a regular courtroom.
"They want to try the case at the foot of the stairwell
in the back of the courthouse," the lawyer said. "they
don't know how to get the wheelchair up the stairs to
the courtroom."

When we arrived we came upon a scene I shall
never forget. The stairwell setting was like something
out of a bizarre horror movie. Several policemen were
standing around. The judge, in his black robes, stood
on the stairs. The prisoner sat slouched in his wheelchair in the center of this incredible scene set against
the dusty, long-unpainted walls of the back hall. I was
later to learn that the police had made young Carl take
off his back supporter because they considered any
such object a dangerous weapon. It did not concern
them that without that support he could not even sit
up straight.

Our attorney was able to get this unique backstairs
trial delayed for an hour so that the lawyer and I could
confer with young Carl and get the facts of what actually happened.

It was obvious from the moment we began talking

to him that young Carl was aware that he was in great
trouble, for most of which he took full responsibility.

Sitting there with us in a big barren room near the
stairs, with police standing outside as if we might all
try to make a getaway, the good-looking, dark-haired
young prisoner who had never had even a traffic viola-
tion on his record before this, frankly and without
trying at all to excuse his own role in the matter, told
us what had happened.

He had had a long day at his office, he explained, and
that was followed by a business dinner meeting with
a client from another company. They had gone to a
nearby restaurant and sat in the cocktail lounge, Carl
in his wheel chair.

The client was accustomed to drinking; Carl was
not. They both had a couple of cocktails as they talked
about business, had another just before dinner and
wine with it. As they were leaving, the client suggested they have a stinger as a nightcap in the lounge.
He was staying right there in the motel connected
with the restaurant. Young Carl had his car outside
and had to drive home.

"I knew I'd had too much," Carl said. "It was my
fault, I blame only myself. In terms of our business
discussions, everything was fine. I had been successful
in accomplishing my goals in our discussion, and I felt
I had done well."

"But by the time I had that final stinger I was not
myself. I didn't know how drunk I actually was. A
normal person would stagger when he stood up to
walk. But I was in a wheel chair. I had no feeling of

being giddy or about to fall. The warning system was not operative. My companion went out with me and put me in the car. I was sure I could get home; there was no heavy traffic and I was only a few miles or so from my home. I would be all right."

"I was wrong. My instincts were right in trying to make a turn about a block from my home but then everything went black on me. The car careened—and this I don't remember—it was told to me afterward. I was driving with hand controls, full hand controls; I'd been doing that for fifteen years. The car made the turn, it hit a stop sign, it went up on the curb, went over the lawn of neighbors, came back down off the curb, kept on for about a city block and came to a halt in somebody's driveway with me slumped over the wheel and the horn blaring away at something like two o'clock in the morning."

Two teen-agers, he told us, heard the horn and called the police. Carl recalled vaguely a scene of flashing red lights and white lights and people talking. His car had run into the back of an empty car parked in the driveway. Neither machine suffered any real damage. The police took a look at Carl, saw the wheel chair and didn't know what to do. They tried to get him out of the car, then discovered that he was physically unable to stand up because of his disability. They also smelled liquor on his breath. They called a police ambulance. At the hospital where they took him a nurse diagnosed his condition as "disabled but under the influence of alcohol."

"I remember then," Carl said, "that one of the po-

The summer day camp at Human Resources Center provides four weeks of fun for severely disabled children from the New York–Long Island area. Some 150 disabled youngsters attend the camp each year.

Dr. Henry "Hank" Viscardi, surrounded by some of the disabled children of Human Resources School, of which he is president. The boat in which they sit has been stabilized and ramped for play by the child in a wheelchair or on crutches.

Designed to complement existing buildings on the campus of Human Resources Center, the new addition to the school will hold an intermediate

learning center for disabled pupils in grades four to six; a new gymnasium; and dining area.

Each of the students accepted by Human Resources School would otherwise be on minimal homebound instruction; at the school, each receives a fully accredited education from pre-school through senior high.

The warmth of a teacher as she reads to her pre-school class helps to make the first few days at school happy ones.

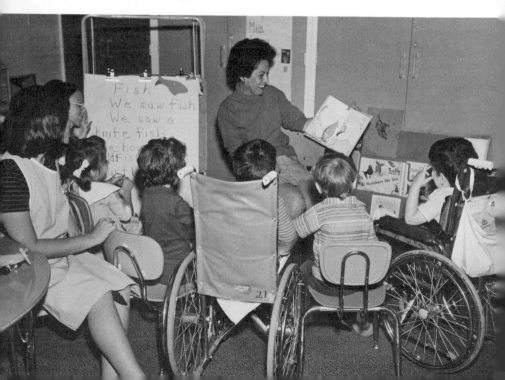

licemen called my mother and told her I was at this hospital and I'd been in an accident and I was being taken to jail on charges of drunken driving and she'd better get some help and come down in the morning. That was all they would tell her. And they hung up.

"Then they put me into a police wagon—they literally lifted me into it bodily and brought me to the police precinct house and took me down to the basement."

His mind began to clear, Carl said, as they carried him into that basement. He realized he was on a stretcher. He asked one of the policemen what had happened. The officer said they'd talk to him when they were ready. Carl asked then if they would lift him into the wheel chair.

They were angry with him, apparently; they virtually threw him into the chair. Then they brought out police forms and began asking questions and taking his statement down as to what he recalled of what had happened. In terms of damage or injury to property or persons, nothing had happened of serious consequence, in actual fact. Nevertheless they were treating this man in a wheel chair almost as they would a hardened habitual criminal.

It was about this time that the real meaning flooded in upon him, Carl said. "I had been intoxicated, even though I had not realized it. I could have killed someone. I would have a police record and very possibly lose my job and wreck my whole career in business. It could affect my whole future life, my fiancée, my engagement. Everything."

They brought in a young man who was handcuffed, angry, and cursing the police. Carl learned later the man had allegedly shot someone with a shotgun. Apparently he'd been in before on other charges and had shot other people. He looked at Carl, then turned to the policeman and asked, "Who's that cripple?" This was to be Carl's companion on the way to the county jail. They lifted Carl up, bodily carried him outside, threw him into the police wagon, and were about to handcuff him to the other man.

"By this time I was absolutely sober, shamed, everything," Carl went on. "I kept trying to explain to them I'd done something wrong, yes. Terribly wrong. But I wasn't a criminal, and I couldn't run away if I wanted to. I tried to explain that I couldn't walk. They didn't have to handcuff me. Without the wheel chair I couldn't move an inch."

Finally, after arguing about it among themselves, they agreed that maybe he didn't have to be handcuffed. By that time it was dawn. And in that bleak moment, riding in the patrol wagon with the handcuffed prisoner sitting across from him, and the police there beside the two prisoners, no one saying anything, with the dawn beginning to light the sky, the whole meaning of this thing that had happened seemed to come crushing in upon him.

The incredible insensitivity of these officers in this situation is almost as inexcusable as their own lack of knowledge in the handling of disabled persons. It was more than mere ignorance or even unconcern; it was almost deliberate sadistic cruelty. This is so often true in situations in which the disabled find themselves.

They had to have known by that time that Carl had no criminal record, that although disabled he was working in an executive position, that he was of good character. Surely all the evidence pointed to the fact that he was no criminal type comparable to the prisoner to whom they had wanted him to be handcuffed.

At the county jail house, they had to lift him out again. There were steep stairs going up into the building. The policemen talked among themselves as to how to get "him" up the stairs. During this discussion, Carl said, they acted as if he were not even there. Several times he started to explain to them what to do but they didn't even let him tell them. After awhile they did listen and he explained that they had to take him up in the wheel chair backwards, on the big wheels, the way you would do with a baby carriage. In that way they got him up the stairs and inside. Heavy black-barred doors clanged shut behind him.

Inside, they took Carl to a dark, dismal room to be fingerprinted and photographed. Usually prisoners stand to have their prints taken but Carl couldn't stand. To get his prints, they actually had to ink the top of one of the lower tables. By that time the police themselves were so upset at this break in the routines that they got the prints confused and had to do it all over again.

There was similar difficulty when he was wheeled into the next room to have a "mug" shot taken. The camera was designed to take prisoners in a standing position. They had to twist and contort the camera angle before the shot could be taken.

After this photographic experience they took him to still another area, the booking room. Here they frisked him up and down. It was here that they discovered the support he had to wear on his body and asked him what it was. I find this one of the most shocking examples I have ever heard of in modern times of heartless and inhumane treatment by public authorities dealing with a disabled person in trouble.

"They felt this support I had to wear and they made me open my clothes and my trousers and take the support off. They also took my belt and my shoes. They apparently did not know or care that when I take that support off I have nothing to support me in the middle—I'm helpless. Sitting in the wheel chair without any support at all is physical agony. But that was the way their rules said it had to be."

It is almost unbelievable to realize the extent of agony to which Carl was put, not because his alleged crime was so heinous but because he happened to belong to the minority for whom life is lived chiefly in a wheel chair.

They wheeled Carl into the section where the cells were—they did not allow him to wheel the chair himself. But when the county jail warden and the guards tried to get the chair through the cell door they discovered the door was too narrow. Most doors are too narrow for wheel chairs.

Carl had to sit there, outside the cell, in the wheel chair. He sat in that one place, in that cell block, immobile in the chair without any support, for three hours, from six-thirty in the morning until nine-thirty, when the strange trial scene in the cell block took place. It was then that I and the attorney I had engaged had arrived.

Just before he was brought in for this trial, young Carl told the attorney, he had been put through another example of the incredible cruelty of official ignorance and unconcern.

"About 9:30 two policemen came in and gave me back my support, my belt, my shoes and that's all, not my personal belongings—not yet. So I sat in the chair and put my support on. Generally you have to do this lying down. I had to do it in a chair and that's almost impossible but I did it. Don't ask me how, but I did. They put me in a police car this time, not a wagon, to take me to the court house.

"At the court house there were more cells where you wait until called. A fellow sitting behind a desk in that cell block said, 'What's that? Get that wheel chair out of here. No wheel chairs in here.' He didn't address this to me. He seemed to be talking to some impersonal object. They took me into a room where a lot of policemen were waiting. I was told to wait there.

"I sat there a half hour or so. Nobody spoke a word to me. Any question about me, what I was doing there, was answered by one of the cops as though I were some inanimate lifeless thing. I think every third or fifth word they used was a curse word.

"An hour-and-a-half later, I was headed for the courtroom. Because the wheel chair couldn't fit up the stairs or through the door into the court, the court officials decided on the stairwell for the trial."

It was as this was about to begin that the attorney and I arrived on the scene and asked for a delay. We got the trial adjourned long enough for us to get the facts, and for our counsel to consider what course to take later that morning when the case resumed in the same improvised stairwell-courtroom.

During that interlude I was waiting too, and I found myself trying to understand the meaning of this senseless and cruel treatment through which Carl had gone. For such treatment wasn't then and is not now unique to police stations and jailhouses and courtrooms. It is indeed a part of the world; it is an attitude, an unconcern that has been a part of mankind for centuries. We have fought it and will go on fighting it. It is part of the task we have given ourselves. I am not advocating that among the public buildings to be freed of architectural barriers we include jails, but surely courthouses; and we could at least develop a procedure to handle persons who are disabled.

Waiting, I recalled earlier days in Washington, with Carl's father, working to help veterans returning from World War II. Many of them were heroes but few of the world outside seemed to care very much then what happened to these men in fulfilling their destiny as ordinary persons in the every day world. A quarter of a century later, I found the same spirit, perhaps even to a greater degree regarding disabled veterans returning from combat in Viet Nam.

I have been told that this is true to such an extent

that some disabled veterans returning from Southeast Asia are hesitant even to discuss how or what action they saw. One young veteran who lost a leg when he stepped on a Viet Cong landmine came to see me in Albertson to talk about possible training for a future role he hoped to play in veterans' rehabilitation. He knew, as well as anyone, the problems of these disabled returnees that no one seemed to care about. "It doesn't matter how you felt about the war—pro or con. These men have done their job, they have paid a price in service to their country. They deserve at least to be treated as human beings by the rest of us."

This from a man who had lost a leg himself in that same blood-drenched struggle.

I thought about his words that day as I waited, and as the strange trial in the stairwell resumed, the words ran in my mind: "At least to be treated as a human being . . ."

The judge stood in his robes on the steps with the District Attorney beside him and Carl in his chair at the foot of the steps. Under our lawyer's guidance, and with the court's consent, Carl was permitted to plead guilty to the minor charge of driving while impaired by alcohol, which is a vehicular not a criminal offense. The penalty imposed by the court was not too severe either: suspension of Carl's license for sixty days.

And outside, Carl's mother and his fiancée were waiting to take him home. For Carl it could well be considered a happy ending to a brief but searing ordeal.

But on the drive back I found my own thoughts

searching for meaning—meaning that went beyond
merely what happened to one young man. To my
mind the case was a glaring symbol of so much else.
It was a symbol of all the things against which we have
been fighting and continue to fight, all the ignorance
of what we are and what we can be, all the prejudice
and superstitious fears, all the unconcern about veterans returning from the battlefields of Indochina. The
barbarities heaped upon one unfortunate paraplegic
trapped in the coils of police authority could be called
his fault, from a legal point of view. But those police,
without knowing it, could have further damaged this
man physically, for the rest of his life, indeed, could
even have cost him his life.

Was this alleged crime, in which no one was hurt,
so serious as to merit such a risk? In any event, it was
one additional fragment in the shifting patterns of the
struggle in which we at Human Resources were
locked.

5

OF MEN AND WOMEN

The Center we established, developed and expanded in Albertson was in large measure designed as an answer to the often total lack of understanding, as well as the frequent mindless cruelties and even barbarity, with which handicapped people are treated even today in these enlightened United States.

Human Resources Center is not a business; it is a research and teaching program—a demonstration of what human beings can do. None of its activities are simply business, not even Abilities which was from the beginning our basic operation. Abilities does many kinds of things commercial, industrial and electronic, and does subcontracting for many organizations. It provides an opportunity for education and training of the disabled while at the same time providing work for many who find it impossible otherwise to get work. It is a headquarters for a cause, a front-line program for the changing of minds and reshaping of thinking and attitudes.

The whole of Human Resources Center is part of this front line, not only Abilities and our research programs, but equally the workshop operations and the school and its programs. And all of these activities had been thrown into a state of turmoil, uncertainty and struggles that had to be dealt with, if we were to survive.

There were forces working for us, and plans going ahead, and there were forces and factors against us. The economic setback in the country at the end of the 1960's was a serious threat to the whole operation of Abilities.

Human Resources Center, although not the first in point of time, is the parent corporation. It is the umbrella which holds together the other branches— Abilities, Human Resources Research and Training Institute, and the Human Resources School. But the real start goes back to Abilities. Everything else springs from that beginning.

Hiring and training disabled people for real jobs back in Abilities' first year of 1952 was a rarity in American industry. The vast complex of our present operation had never even been dreamed of then. The original Abilities was launched in a vacant garage in West Hempstead. We had to go out and scrounge for work; we had to improvise techniques for production, techniques by which our disabled people could be trained. We were at the start a mere five people with five good arms and one good leg in the whole lot. But we learned, we produced and the work came in.

Art Nierenberg who has been with us from the beginning, and who was to become president of Abilities under the new Human Resources Center set up in

1970, was one of the original group in the West Hempstead garage. "I recall the frustrations of those early
days as we searched our way," Art told me once. "We
didn't have the answers ourselves and yet somehow
we got the job done. I'm also aware that a lot of times
it was prayer more than anything else that seemed to
give us answers."

Some of what Art was saying and recalling had its
amusing sidelights: "I remember," he said, "eighteen
years ago when you came back with some new order
for business and somebody wanted a purchase order
to give us some material and you didn't know what
such a purchase order was and neither did any of the
rest of us. It wasn't even in the dictionary. But there
were many who wanted to help and we got answers
finally. Those were the first months, the first beginnings. The Korean War was on and we began to get
orders from aircraft companies, for wiring harnesses
and electronic components, packaging, and small assembly operations."

A few years later, we moved into the new building
in Albertson—right into the heart of an area which at
that time was rural, semi-rural at least, reasonably
undeveloped, and we set out to buy the land and build
something permanent, beautiful, to keep the rural
effect. This was when there were still only a handful
of houses around us, and we encountered our first
opposition in the unsuccessful attempt to stop us from
constructing the first building.

Abilities had grown and continued to grow rapidly
from its garage beginnings. It was already heralding

a whole new era for the disabled, a new kind of opportunity for disabled people to work and produce. It had to do more. There were many things we had to learn about what was happening to this new brand of workers. Did they get better or worse with time? How could we train them? What was their attitude, their motivation? Emotionally, they were more or less controlled and stable, through the work they were now doing, as compared to the time when, from an occupational point of view, they were virtual shut-ins.

What psychological changes occurred in cardiacs who were considered unemployable? What tools and jigs and fixtures were needed to make almost totally disabled people productive workers? What bio-engineering and bio-mechanical devices were needed to train and improve their compensatory capacities to work?

All of these questions in those beginning days were part of uncertain areas still to be probed. And one concept developed quite early at Abilities was that an important part of our job was to begin this exploration. We had to know more about the disabled at work. Out of the workshop called Abilities there would have to come a research and training center where we could share the knowledge with others, and could continue to accumulate more knowledge about the physically handicapped.

This program began in 1954, only two years after Abilities was founded. Our first medical director was so shocked when he came to examine workers at Abilities and saw the kind of people we employed that he wanted to quit. In fact, he tried to quit on the very first day but we prevailed on him to stay for a time at least.

Nothing was easy in those days but we and our medical examiner somehow did survive. Even the evolution of names wasn't easy. The name "Abilities, Inc." was a natural. But then we had to develop a new name for the research aspect. For that we came up with a corporate name of "Human Resources Engineering" only to learn from Albany that we couldn't do that. In the first place the engineers had a watchdog group that kept tabs on such matters and got laws passed by which non-engineers had no right to use the word in a name unless they really were actual engineers with a degree and license to prove it. The watchdog contingent resented barbers calling themselves "tonsorial engineers," or cleaning people calling themselves "clothes engineers."

We called our research center, which included physical therapy equipment and a swimming pool, "Human Resources Foundation." That seemed to be all right with Albany, so we chartered under that name in Albertson. To our shock, however, almost at once we began to get letters from people asking us, "How do we get a grant of money from your foundation? And by the way, how much do you give per individual grant?" The whole thing was a traumatic experience. We don't give grants, we try to get them.

The misunderstanding grew worse, rather than better. Some of those writing to the Foundation trying to get funds took exception to our statement that we had no money to give out to anybody. We had to get a protective new approach to hold off hungry seekers of funds we didn't have. Then the foundation to whom we appealed for funds wanted an explanation. They did not give to other foundations, they explained in reply to our appeals for grants. It was most confusing.

That was how the all-embracing term "Human Resources Center" was born. At first we simply dropped the word "Foundation" and chartered as "Human Resources." Then when the Human Resources School was chartered we decided to place all of the operations under Human Resources Center.

Obviously, workers at Abilities are the subject of research and obviously that research is of value to disabled workers and work programs in America, in Australia, in Japan, in fact, throughout the world.

At the same time, Abilities has to stand alone. It must, out of its own earnings, support itself. We have from the first day insisted on paying prevailing wages, insisted that Abilities receive no subsidy. Equally, the Human Resources School must operate as an educational corporation, separate from the other activities at the Center, yet a part of the same family and under the same roof. Each relates to the Human Resources Research and Training Institute. The disabled child finds himself studying in an environment where there are successful disabled adults, where there is a constant search for new knowledge which will affect his life.

How profound has Abilities become in the depth of its operations? In terms of total production, there have been some years, not many, when the total value of goods produced reaches several million dollars. There have been other years when there were losses but the good years allowed for reserve funds to make up for the bad. Abilities operates strictly as a non-profit workshop center. In the nearby community of Syosset it has a separate Packaging Department, employing another thirty-five persons.

Abilities has, in fact, a number of departments, including Data Processing, Electronics, Research and Product Development Engineering, Banking, and, just as in any well-run work center, a host of subdivisions, a complex of activities. The Glass Department, for example, turns out carved glassware. President Johnson, with the guidance of the First Lady, selected one of our patterns to be used as the official gift from the President to foreign visitors.

Is Abilities a success, a triumph? Perhaps. But many of our friends do not know the heartbreak, the day-to-day uncertainties, the cutbacks. We, too, had to go through the declines when the economic cycle broke, when our contracts and sub-contracts ran out. Abilities reflects in its own way the general economy. When it is up we are up. We are no different from anyone else. This means in our own precision specialties we can match the work, performance for performance, dollar for dollar, can match or even exceed what non-disabled workers turn out. It means that we accept our risks and setbacks just like anyone else who works and produces. These, after all, are the terms we ourselves insisted on, to be the same as, not different from, other workers.

In the months followng the Korean War, a recession began to spread across America—particularly across Long Island, which was built largely on a defense-production, military-hardware economy. There were severe economic changes, cut-backs in defense production. The major contract we held at that time was with aircraft and military-component manufacturers. Better than ninety per cent of our work was being drawn under contracts with them. We were fully aware of the peril of having that large a percentage of our workload with such customers. But we had to take these workload contracts as and where and when. In any case, we were too young and inexperienced to make a turn-around to a new type of operation.

We and our people, our Abilities workers, numbering at that time 350 handicapped men and women in the workshop itself, were once again at the low rung of the economic situation. As the contracts ran out there were no renewals. People all over the Island were being laid off. We ourselves—Abilities—began laying off men and women who were doing a tremendous job as long as the work assignment was there. With the work fading, they knew, better than anyone outside, how hard it would be to find other employment in other places. These were the heads of families, men and women, many of whom had found their first jobs—after years of searching and trying—at Abilities. We had to begin to lay these people off because there was no work to do, no contracts to fulfill. We were caught with no reserves of money and with debts to be paid. It was a very trying time, and we almost went under.

But we survived that post-Korean era. We survived because of a spirit that is something extra in people. We survived because concerned people in the community came forth to help us refinance mortgages and consolidate debts while we regrouped to face a changing economy. We survived and grew and our precision production came to be accepted by the industrial community and respected for its conscientious work, its attention to controls, details, to exactitude in production. Because of our very limitations, there was need for greater care, greater urgency, greater effort, the greatest conscientiousness built into the final product. We survived because we were willing to meet the changing times and sought to build a better product at a fair price with quality and delivery dates on target.

I recall another kind of job we had, in another moment of crisis in later years. This was with the Litton Systems, Inc. In the midst of the struggle in Viet Nam, one of the top people at Litton Systems, Inc. came to see us and decided that our earlier work in electronic products had given us a special know-how. This could be of value to Litton and perhaps to the nation's military effort. One item our people had to set up in the plant was a special test laboratory for difficult and exacting projects. We accomplished this by converting a former lunch cafeteria into a laboratory where computer flight navigation equipment was tested under exact atmospheric and temperature and pressure conditions. The same equipment would be subjected to flight conditions at 30,000 feet or better. Litton produced the test equipment and the technicians and Abilities provided the work force of skilled individuals who had made us known for extremely fine, demanding detail work calling for almost infinite patience, motivation and concern. Our job was to rebuild this equipment after it had flown a specified period of time. We were the retrofit team for Litton and the Navy.

We met the demands, the needs; we readjusted our own work schedules. We agreed to work overtime; Litton agreed to let us establish extra shifts, any and all hours, full overtime or not. Of course workers were paid overtime and doubletime. There was occasionally work on weekends. Our supervisors took trips to the West Coast as required, often on short notice, to take part in conferences that soon became known as "Red-Eye Specials" because of the strain, the lack of sleep.

At the workshop, with our own people, there was an almost unbelievable spirit. Work that would take others six months to carry out, we were doing with equal or better performance in thirty-five calendar days. We heard stories that the Marine squadron leaders, when given a choice of having equipment from some other group or from Abilities, preferred the equipment from Abilities because of the quality and the high performance of the work itself.

We did well in that emergency assignment. And we were ahead financially and providing employment to our people. But as the cutbacks set in, as the economy of the Sixties began to falter, as the inflationary leap-frog to disaster went on, Abilities itself was again in trouble.

Our work with Litton Systems, Inc. began to recede. They promised us new contracts but they had problems also and the day came when we had no work from Litton at all. Other customers were affected for similar reasons. Long Island was a disaster area economically. All firms cut back. Unemployment soared. Many small companies closed their doors. It was a real recession.

We held out as long as possible. Then began the inevitable thought of layoffs. Overnight, it seemed, three fourths of our production had shut down.

It was the old lesson of the Korean War. But this time we were better prepared. We had tucked away surplus funds for such a moment and with the help of our Board sought to bring in new management skills and develop new programs and services to vie for the available work. We needed engineering and marketing services if we were going to get new business, new products, new workloads. We developed a whole new electronic capacity of servicing the equipment of other companies. We had already gained experience in this through our test laboratory work for Litton. Now with our own engineering group we were ready to do this for the Navy, the Army, or for any of the large corporations that required this kind of servicing of computerized and electronic equipment. We sought to expand our banking and data processing departments and to develop a product line of our own.

But the recession was longer and worse than expected, work came in slowly and the times grew economically chill. Abilities had to stand on its own feet. Yet it was not our purpose to exact a price of people, to go down the list and see where and how the layoffs had to be. Perhaps it would come to that but we were not about to surrender as the depth of a new recession appeared to be taking hold at the end of the 1960's. As the work diminished, people were shifted about. Those who left were not replaced. No new workers were hired. Then the work week was cut to thirty hours. In the course of those months we lost more than five hundred thousand dollars.

It was also vitally important to retain our capacity to fight back. New work had to be engineered first, by a team which had reputation and belief in its capacity. We were not alone in the fight. I thank God that Art and his team, backed by the Abilities Board, had prepared as soundly as humanly possible for this life-or-death struggle.

6

OF BOYS AND GIRLS

‖‖‖

The other side of the story at Human Resources concerned not adults and work opportunities but children and their struggle for the right, the opportunity, to participate in the educational process.

From the beginning we knew how difficult and challenging this would be. We knew that we and the faculty we brought together were moving into uncharted educational fields. We knew that with some of these boys and girls the physical challenge might present great difficulty. But we believed—and have since demonstrated—that we could meet these challenges, so that these children could learn and grow to the fullest extent possible.

I am talking about the most extremely physically disabled children, congenitally or otherwise, in the world—the paraplegic, the child born without legs or arms, the child born with some rare disease that may allow him or her only a diminishing handful of disabled years compared to the normal life span. Should we teach such children as these? Should we not hide them away, as some of our friends might wish? There are many like them. But do not these children have a right to their years, however limited? Should they not be allowed like everyone else to participate, to learn, as long as they can, as much as they can, to laugh, to swim, to triumph, even to dream?

In the past, and even now in many parts of the world, the severely handicapped child is often hidden. Some still are kept in an upstairs bedroom that becomes almost a prison. This is the child the neighborhood hears about but does not often see. It is the strange one "up there on the second floor," the small lonely face peeking through the window at the world outside.

Our school opened that window, opened the doors of the real world for children like these. We explored and developed the techniques by which they could go to school, by which their problems could be dealt with properly and successfully. In the early days of the school, we went out and searched for these hidden children, met and talked with their parents, explained to them why they had no reason to fear, and why and how these children could achieve, could learn to work and play and study.

We built a complex, sophisticated and uniquely designed school for these children. From a handful in our first class, the school has grown to a waiting list of scores. From children who formerly never saw the world except from that upstairs window of their earlier lives they have become youngsters who travel widely across the community, who have seen and toured great museums and historic places, have been backstage at TV shows, have travelled to colleges and ball games and theatres, have seen and heard and touched the beauty of the world. Many have gone on to the campuses of colleges and universities after graduation.

It was a group of these children, from the high school classes, we took by bus to Albany to see the operations of the state government at the capitol. And it was here that the legislators stood and acknowledged these children with a standing ovation, and made speeches from the floor praising the work of these children and their school. It was for all of us an exciting, dramatic moment when those spontaneous cheers rang out. I actually saw tears in the eyes of our lady volunteers.

What are they like, these young people of our school? Essentially, they are like everybody else. They come from homes of all types; they do the same things generally that all children do, good and bad, noisy and quiet. I remember on one trip, one of our very bright youngsters was asked what she wanted for dinner. She had been told she could have whatever she liked. While the rest of us had shrimp cocktail to start, she ordered cake and ice cream, then worked her way backward through the main course, all the way down to the shrimp and olives for dessert. For many the restaurant with its menu was a new experience.

On another occasion—I believe it was on the Albany trip—the children were told in the restaurant where they were taken that they could have anything on the breakfast menu that struck their fancy. Our headmaster who made this lavish pronouncement assumed that our angels would take it easy and no one would go for more than bacon and eggs with, perhaps, toast on the side. But a couple of the more astute students went for what was called the Executive Breakfast. This, listed at $4.95, included not only eggs but also steak and potatoes.

Of course we have our people with the students throughout the trip—our volunteers, some of them college students, our nurse, our faculty. All share in caring for the children, watching them, tending their needs, whatever those needs may be, helping with their toilet problems if needed, or turning a muscular dystrophy child from one side to the other at regular intervals through the night, so that the child can sleep in comfort.

I am always amazed and grateful to our faculty and our teachers' aides for their enthusiasm in volunteering for these trips and for their love of our wonderful children. This enthusiasm is contagious. It provides the thrust which moves obstacles and accomplishes impossible objectives. Our children's hunger for love calls forth the sort of love in the name of which men have dreamed great dreams and achieved heroic deeds. It is a love that grows greater—as exemplified in both our parents and our faculty—with that hunger and that need.

There are always problems, and they almost always are resolved. Interesting problem on the Albany trip: Most of the doors on the lavatories at the motels were too narrow for a wheelchair to get through. But we found ways. In some instances we got out a screw driver, took off the wheels and slid the chair the rest of the way. In other cases we simply took off the hinges and temporarily removed the lavatory door. But we always put it back in place properly before we left.

What I like to remember about that Albany trip isn't the hundred and one problems really. It is all the other factors—the factor of this participation in life. A participation not of children we are supposed to pity, but of young people fulfilling themselves as all children do, sharing a picnic lunch at a rest area along the New York Thruway, taking part in a hundred other activities of life and learning what once had been considered impossible for them.

Millions of children, disabled or not, are being irreparably damaged by our failure to stimulate their intellectuality during their crucial years, the earliest years of their lives, the pre-school years. Millions are being held back from their true potential. This is another form of disability.

To me one of the most glaring defects of our educational system is that it does not prepare the student for life. Instead of involving the disabled child who is able to go to public school in actual life problems, for example, it takes him away from these problems.

Much of my effort has been and continues to be spent in raising funds needed to run the research, training and education operations, with considerable emphasis on funds for the construction of the new school building. Many magnificent gifts have been made, and as we approached the end of 1970, we had raised all but $300,000 of the needed $3,500,000 to complete the new building, the parking area, and landscaping, and for the establishment of a sound endowment fund to support the building. It is a task of people—planners, leaders, teachers, volunteers, parents, pupils, contributors, builders, designers. These are the people who shape the plans for our students and their future.

How grateful I am for the belief in us by so many persons who have made these efforts possible.

Let me talk about two of our children—a boy and a girl—one of whom, the girl, was on that incredibly wonderful journey to Albany and shared that moment when the acknowledgement resounded across the Senate and Assembly in the state capitol. They happened to be a boy and girl with widely differing destinies.

Paul is a very young man who lives on a litter. He has serious physical disabilities. He was born with osteogenesis imperfecta, a congenital disease in which the bones are abnormally brittle and subject to fractures. This can occur as early as in intra-uterine life and is frequent in early childhood and young adulthood. To protect his brittle structure, Paul is in a body cast from his chest to his toes. It is to him what a shell is to a turtle. He can move about only on a litter on wheels which he propels himself. It is, in effect, his home. For many years Paul was not allowed to go to school; he was one of those to whom the world was a largely unknown arena. Then he learned about our school, began to attend it, and not only was able to keep up with the work in class but became one of the real leaders in the school.

When he was graduated from Human Resources School, he went on to Hofstra University, on Long Island, a learning center which has pioneered in developing new aids for the disabled student, such as ramps, instead of stairs, wider aisles to allow for wheelchair traffic, elevators, special accoustical aids, and other devices. Paul intends to be a lawyer; he may even go into politics. He is president of our alumni association. He has already become one of the leaders here in college activities. He was elected president of the student council. His voice is heard and his cogent arguments for his cause listened to. Other students help him in areas where he needs help. If there is a class inaccessible to him for physical reasons, or there are stairs to climb to reach a classroom, or for some reason he can not leave his dorm, they bring him their notes and their assignments.

Here is a youth who belonged to the category of the forgotten—the ones that they used to hide away. Yet one day this highly successful young college student may be practicing law in our State and Federal courts. Paul is already a triumph and his work and career are only at the starting line.

There is also the story of Shari. Sharon was her real name. But everyone always called her Shari. Shari was suffering from a severe disability, indeed several disabilities. Most of her life she was in a wheelchair. She had what is called, medically, dysautonomia, a disease which effects the autonomic nervous system.

There is physical incoordination and a weakening of the reflexes. The body is small in early adulthood. There is difficulty in swallowing and breathing. The person cannot cry because the tear duct control is attrited. Tactile sensation is greatly impaired.

It was obvious that a severe spasm could come during the night at any time—and if it did, if it was too serious, if it could not be brought under control, Shari would die. In spite of her young years, she would simply run out of vital capacity for life. These children do not live beyond their teens.

Yet she was such a normal, wonderful girl—despite her physical problems; alert, bright, eager to learn, eager to be a part of this world so close at hand and so far away. Before our school was started she had no school to which she could go, of course. No one was prepared to take the responsibility in any normal educational situation, nor could she cope with the physical environment of a regular school. Her disability was too great. She needed a wheel chair among other things.

Most of her life Shari stayed at home. On certain days she would get up in the morning and wait for her home-bound tutor, provided by the local school district. There was not really enough time to study in the sense of education for something beyond. Once a week for several hours is not enough instruction for the eager mind of a youngster who wants to learn. It was not education at all; it was hardly even escape.

She did manage to go to some special education classes, but as her mother put it, "She learned virtually nothing. The teacher was more of a baby sitter than anything else. Like other disabled children she was not allowed to participate in any of the other school activities. They sat in the classroom from morning to mid-afternoon, mostly doing nothing."

Shari heard about our school, and this bright, wonderful child who lived so close to the edge and who wanted so much to know and taste some of the meaning of life, came into the school, and grew up with it. She became one of its most popular students. This school and its people, its students and teachers—this was her wonderful world of which she became part, in which she learned and thrived and delighted.

"The school is the most important part of her life," Shari's mother told me once. "This is where she first met the world, she grew up with it, she was accepted here, she'd come in and Eileen Kramer at the front desk would say, 'There's Shari, she's the best kid on the block.'

"And everyone would come up to her, you know. Alex with his little half-stumps for arms and legs would come by to kiss his girl in the morning. I can't begin to tell you where it begins and where it ends— it's a complete life. And then to come home from school and talk to the other girls—the neighbors' children who drop in—and she would tell them, 'I'm studying this or I am learning that in my school.' "

Once, the mother said, Shari went to a wedding. The first she'd ever been to. The groom happened to be French and Shari had now learned to speak French in our school and when she heard the bridegroom speaking French she wheeled over to him and called out to him in her quiet, slightly difficult way of speaking, "Bonne chance . . . bonne chance."

That was Shari—Shari who came to our school and became one of our youngsters and grew up with her class and did many of the things all children do, and into young womanhood, and perhaps because she knew that there was a time limit, sometime for her, she drank in life with a warmth and excitement that won the hearts of everyone who knew her.

One non-disabled whose life became involved with Shari is a handsome youth everyone calls E.J. His name is actually E.J. Hahn, a college student, who came originally to work with our kids in our summer camp program, conducted on a kind of informal way on the grounds and in the buildings of our school, with numerous side trips in the school buses. E.J. is interested in religion and philosophy. Once he felt he might go into the clergy himself. He was one of the faculty for the elective classes on religion. "I base my lecture on the *Gospel According to Peanuts.* It's different, but the kids understand it."

Our summer faculty is composed entirely of high school senior and college undergraduate students, many of whom, like E.J., come back during the fall and winter to complete their student-teaching assignments.

Of course E.J. met and knew Shari. In mid-summer there was a staff meeting of the camp leaders and counsellors, and Shari told them how much she enjoyed camp and she added that she wouldn't normally want to go to camp because she was so much older than most of the kids—she was now twenty-one years old. Because of her dysautonomia, she looked younger, and smaller, in her wheel chair.

But she had gone to the camp director, Rick McCarthy, and asked him if she could become a counsellor-in-training next summer and Rick said of course she could. She was accepted as a junior counsellor. So she was really excited about the camp program and what was happening over the summer, and she was very happy. On Friday night, following the staff meeting, there was to be a staff party and Shari and her mother were invited to attend.

This was to be at a restaurant where there was a band and dancing and dinner. Shari had to be there. She was the only student allowed at the party. But it was summertime and Shari was treated as a member of the faculty anyway.

E.J. related to me in his own words the story of that night:

"One thing Shari always wanted was to be treated just like a lady, just like the rest of the 21-year-old girls who were at the party. Her mother wasn't feeling well and told Shari, 'I don't think I'm going to be able to go tonight.' And Shari was all upset and told her mother, 'Mommy, you *have* to go!' Her mother had a cup of hot tea, and she was feeling better, and they went home to change.

"It was a nice party at the restaurant. Shari and her mother and I and Alex and the summer nurse were sitting at one table and the rest of the staff were sitting around; the whole thing was set up as a kind of U-shaped table. Everyone came about nine o'clock and the band started playing about ten. Shari was thoroughly enjoying the evening, and we just sat and talked about camp, and what a great time camp was this summer, what a really fantastic program.

"Shari's mother said she was feeling better, still a little queasy but for Shari's sake she was so glad she had come. Just before they arrived they got lost on the parkway coming in and she said Shari told her she'd have to call me and find out how to get there. So we went and picked them up at a service station where they were waiting for us. And just before she left the party, Shari and I danced. She in her wheel chair and I on my feet, but we swirled around. She had a good time; she enjoyed it, she was smiling."

Wheel chair dancing, even in square dances, is not uncommon in our school. In fact with the unusual body motions of modern dancing our youngsters have a great time in their wheel chairs.

About a quarter to twelve, Shari's mother told her, "I think it's time to go home, Shari." And Shari said goodnight to her friends, and they started outside. The car was parked in the driveway. Somebody asked E.J. if he'd go along to make sure everything was all right.

"As we were going out of the building," E.J. continued, "Shari said, 'Mommy, I feel a little dizzy.' She was walking the short distance to the car while we folded her wheel chair. And then she passed out—right outside the restaurant, about five steps from the

Individual attention, utilizing volunteers—students from local colleges and high school as well as housewives—makes it possible for the disabled student to receive a maximum of individual attention.

The worlds of art and music—often inaccessible to the child confined to a wheelchair—are brought to Human Resources School through specially arranged programs, in which the artist or musician demonstrates his particular skill and encourages participation by the students.

A full range of business and vocational courses are provided in Human Resources School, including coursework in the field of data processing and computer science.

The Lilco Laboratory for everyday living is designed to complement the normal course of study in Human Resources School. If the disabled student is to become a self-supporting adult, he will need to learn concepts of self-care and independent living.

Independent supervised research encourages the disabled student to follow his own interests under the guidance of the specially trained teaching personnel.

Disabled students are normally excluded from science courses simply because they cannot safely utilize the equipment and chemicals involved. At Human Resources School modifications in the desks and in some of the laboratory equipment have made the lab a safe place in which to learn on a par with students in public school.

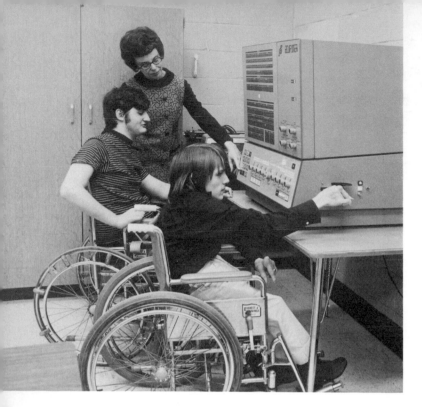

Individual study and instruction is made possible through the use of programmed tapes and equipment. The machine pictured above is used in teaching disabled students concepts of data processing and console operation.

Each of the classrooms in Human Resources School is equipped with up-to-date teaching aids which take into consideration the physical limitations faced by someone in a wheelchair. This class is learning computer keypunching through the use of an overhead projecting device.

doorway. She said she felt dizzy, so I grabbed her, and she slid down and I picked her up and carried her to the car. I put her on the seat of the car and then I went and got the camp nurse and she said, when she arrived there, that she didn't even get a pulse. Shari was gagging but I think it was really only an automatic nervous reaction.

"We rushed her to Nassau Hospital. Rick McCarthy was giving Shari artificial respiration and mouth-to-mouth resuscitation in the back seat as I drove the car. Shari's mother was with us. The camp nurse went in her own car, leading the way for us to the hospital. The doctors told us Shari was dead on arrival. But I already knew she was dead."

There is an important epilogue to this story, an epilogue in love. For all the people around her, all the people who knew her and loved her, knew also, as she did, that this was going to happen, that it could happen at any instant, that sooner or later it would happen. But between that sooner and later there was life itself, there was learning, there was doing, there was living the life of a young girl in school with her teachers and friends.

Did not Shari have a right, like any other human being, any other lovely young lady, to all of this, no matter how short or how long the time itself might be in terms of average human measurement?

Shari's mother understood. She told me of her gratitude for everything that everyone tried to do that night. She was particularly grateful that E.J. had asked Shari to dance. "When would any young man ask her to dance?" she was saying. "Because she was dancing in her wheel chair."

And she told how E.J. had looked, so vibrant and handsome, and how Shari had moved her head up and down in time to the music.

"It was a wonderful moment," Shari's mother said. "It was her moment. She was delighted, she was accepted, she was happy."

I think of this and the other aspects of the story of the school—our plans to expand the school's service to the community and to the disabled. And I think of the opposition to these plans, I think of the people who insist they love little girls like Shari—but not on our block.

What was it then that these neighbors were opposing, and for which they solicited funds from door to door to hire lawyers, and held meetings and threshed about in their eagerness to halt our program which admittedly centered largely around these children?

When we began, Human Resources School was in one room—a room later turned into a research laboratory. It was a modern version of the little red schoolhouse with everything and everyone thrown into one room, classes first to eighth. Then we built our first school building, with much planning and concern, and included in it such things as the laboratory for everyday living—learning how to make a bed or get in and out of bed even though disabled, to take a shower or a bath alone, to cook and sew, to develop skills to live as fully normal lives as possible. That was a part of the first building. Beginning with only a few classes we gradually expanded into a full pre-school-through-high-school program. Although our youngest students come in at age three, no one lives at the school. All must come in school buses each day.

We had made the decision to build this original school building as an addition to our center and we added more classrooms as we grew. But we also made the decision not to launch drives for massive numbers of students. I believed that the limit should be approximately 200 students; our purpose has never been to provide the answer to all crippled children but to develop techniques and practical teaching methods that others could carry on and expand in educational facilities across the nation.

Our job was to do the special education research, the curriculum pioneering, to train teachers in this new avenue of teaching. It was also to cope with and understand in depth the physical, psychological and emotional problems, to record and document and share all the information and findings with others.

So we had a school. For that school we needed but had not built a gymnasium or a cafeteria. Older students have been allowed to eat in the Abilities cafeteria. But it is also true that many of these children have special deficiencies and require special nutriments that are not found in a regular lunch however solid or healthful for average people.

We couldn't build a gym for these children at the start for the reason that neither we nor any other group knew exactly what the requirements of such a gym would be nor could we have afforded it. What kind of adapted physical education program would serve our difficult needs? How should our children participate in such programs? What kind of games could we teach these youngsters to play?

Five years later, we had learned the answers to these questions. Our people knew what kind of physical exercise, what sort of games were right. The programs of these years with our adapted physical education experiments had provided many of the answers. So we had to build a new building on our grounds, in which there would be a gymnasium and also a cafeteria, designed with all the beauty and skill of the finest architects, to fit into the need inside and the pattern of our community outside. A second floor would house a computer setup, primarily for educational purposes. Computers present a magnificent new field of opportunity, one of the great areas for the disabled because it does not require tremendous physical strength or excessive motion. The plans also included the underground parking garage that would make it unnecessary to have large numbers of cars in the open around the building and would also make it possible for the disabled to be brought directly into the building in elevators, particularly important in inclement weather.

The whole area above this garage was planned to be landscaped and this would be combined with the twenty acres we own into a beautiful campus park, which would be of value not only to the children but also would enhance the entire neighborhood.

Because of the nature of the school and its purposes

we believe deeply in developing new techniques. A special grant was obtained, for example, from the Heckscher Foundation for Children, to build an electronics-game area. The functions of physical and occupational therapy are such that they can be made exciting and different—not merely routine—so that the children will want to do them. Our plan is to give them the excitement of games in an amusement park.

We believe, for instance, that we can use pinball machines and slot machines, not for gambling but for therapy. The youngster who plays pinball baseball, for example, will be getting special hand- and arm-muscle use and exercise that is vital to his capacity but that so many youngsters find not too interesting if presented to them as a straight exercise. Slot machines with their one-armed-bandit setup are a promising alternate. Our plan is to reprogram the slot machine so that the youngsters would be opposing pitchers on a baseball team or quarterbacks in a football game. The operation of the levers would be adjusted to provide the exercise and could be prescribed according to the needs of the individual.

I did run into a major problem, however, regarding implementation of this plan. I was also advised that under Federal law it is illegal to transport slot machines across state lines for any purpose whatsoever. And the best place to obtain them is in Las Vegas. I am at this writing in touch with friends in the field and prominent legal counsel in New York City to see what if any special dispensations we might be able to get for using the machines for our special purposes.

I haven't quite joined the mob. But there are days when I have wondered.

These, then, are the building plans which we have developed. This is the "ugly factory" we are constructing, the potential five-story "skyscraper" that is going to destroy the property values.

Shari's mother has told me that it comforts her that Shari had our school, our facilities, our approach, because otherwise she would have felt that her child had had nothing. "What did she have? What was her life? It would have been nothing without this place, this school, that gave her a purpose, a joy in life."

I could not wash away the tears of that mother. I could only reaffirm how much Shari had meant to us, how much we loved her.

"The hours in the schoolroom," I told Shari's mother, "the affection of their teachers, the lessons we can give the children for their future lives—all this is a miracle too in its way, for a lifetime, an hour, even one moment of life that is wholly theirs."

7

OF BLACK AND WHITE

There is an affinity among all minority groups, an underlying response to each other's needs. Regardless of where he finally manages to go to school, the crippled child or the black child is almost certain to have a special cross to bear, especially in the frightened world of the American suburb.

I recall one morning, at a time when we were locked in this battle with the neighborhood group, I received a phone call from a man who identified himself as a black post-graduate college student at a nearby university. He had read in the newspapers about the actions some of the residents were trying to take against us. "If you want any help you'll get it from us," he assured me. "You tell me to go ahead—when and where. We'll do the rest."

I believe too deeply in our government, our laws and our courts to turn to any real activist approach, whatever was in the young man's mind. Yet I understood his feelings, his reasons, and I thanked him and said I hoped the possibility or need for anything of that nature would never arise.

It was only one of a number of similar calls I received in these weeks. The black people, too, were locked in struggle. They too found themselves battling local prejudices and petitions and mass meetings to prevent a new housing project or a new food program in the local high school. Many such protests did appear to be directed primarily at policies and programs which would be of particular benefit to black people seeking to establish new lives for themselves and their families in suburban communities.

In New Hyde Park, one of the nearby communities under the jurisdiction of the town of North Hempstead, blacks had been involved also in the proposed new educational-cultural zoning plan. Things were in considerable ferment there, too. In that instance they were backing a proposed middle-income housing project, very much needed and worthwhile.

Months before this, many New Hyde Park residents had insisted that the land involved in that community be zoned for low-density residential purposes only—as a buffer against an industrial-commercial zoning. However, when the proposal came to build on this property a middle-income high density residential project which would be predominantly black, organized elements of the community at once reversed this stand on residential land use and insisted the area had to be rezoned as commercial or industrial.

Numerous calls came to us from both blacks and whites concerned about various local situations involving this kind of tug of war. Young people in college and high school also wrote and called. Many of these were students who knew about our school and our summer camping program on the grounds. These young people were way out. They were ready to picket Town Hall, they said. Just give the signal, Mr. Viscardi, and we'll march, one of them told us over the phone.

I had considered such a course in one of our darker moments, but—as already noted in this book—I had held back. It simply is not our way. Nor am I convinced that any direct action of itself is going to change things for us or any of these other groups. We each have to deal with our own needs—and each is essentially its own unique situation.

The situation of the disabled, for example, I believe will take longer to change than will that of the blacks. The problem of the black people has had far wider exposure and discussion and I believe it will be solved sooner than that of the handicapped.

The tragic black, the most tragic in many ways, is the disabled black, the black man in the wheel chair. No one wants him or appears to care what happens to him. None of the federal or state programs for the economically deprived includes the disabled as such. White or black, they are excluded and among the poor or the black they are too often forgotten.

We have many of them in the workshop at Abilities and are particularly saddened when they must be laid off because of the recession and lack of work in the shop. There is rarely another job waiting for them, even when times are good.

For the non-disabled black people, their social and economic situations have made their point clear. It is not only the whites who have fled the cities. It is also the blacks. In tens of thousands of cases, the moment a black family can, it moves out of the city slums and all that has held him hostage. Both groups have fled the same urban blight. Both have become invaders of the shopping center paradise, each seeking their escape.

Blacks as well as whites have found a place in the suburbs but the black people have had to battle for it step by step, block by block.

One of our own black workers came to me during this period when both the black community and the disabled were locked each in its own separate struggle. He asked if he could come in and see me. I had known him for some time. Indeed, he was one of our best workers, although he was a wheel chair-bound paraplegic.

What he was suggesting was that we join forces outright, the blacks and the disabled. "We blacks are up in arms about this thing about the housing. Nobody cares about blacks except blacks. And nobody cares at all about the disabled black, do they? Not even most of the blacks themselves."

We talked about this problem, there in my office. Most of it had to do with the fact that black people had difficulty getting any kind of real work. "Think of the employer who doesn't want to hire black workers anyway," he said. "Then think of the same employer who's asked to hire a handicapped black person without arms or legs and usually without education and all the other things he's been deprived of because of being a black person."

He sat there across from my desk, looking out my window at the early winter landscape and the cold blustering blue sky of that winter day. He and I had ties that went back a long way. He said slowly, "If you're interested in having a real march and a real hoe-down in front of that town hall, I want to tell you, there are an awful lot of black people who are waiting for you to say let's go. In fact there are a lot of our people so incensed we may go without you."

I said, "Charlie, you've been here for ten years. You know I don't run from a fight. We're going to win— you can count on that. But there are other ways."

"I can't agree with you," he said. "I think you'd better show all that muscle." Then he smiled. "When you're ready, you say the word because I'd be glad to be right at the head of that parade—right at your side."

And the other side—the active minorities of the opposition—was always on call. In a world that is always too busy, too pressed for time, it is only the few who are able to take a day or a week off to organize the protesters against a day-care center or a library, to raise funds for some lawyer to shout and abuse and denounce, always for carefully developed pseudo-reasons—those who oppose such things as schools, nurseries and libraries.

What do these people who fight really stand for? In a certain way of which they are perhaps themselves unaware, they have a new land of escape, privately established segregation not so much against any individual minority as against whatever is new, whatever is different, whatever may hold a challenge to their citadel.

Analyzing this situation, one leading Long Island psychologist was quoted in the local press as believing that people in Long Island appeared to be trying "to buy themselves an enclave" with their own kind, where they always know what to expect every day. "It is our most primitive way of relating," the psychologist declared. "Any change represents a threat, and so people become oversensitive to change."

This is part of what lies behind the stormy zoning hearings, and bitter and aggressive protests against any proposal to feed children, to teach children, to provide a new facility for children in their midst who are different in any way. This has been true of buildings for the retarded, the emotionally disturbed, even housing for the aged.

Of course, in all of this, black people have taken the heaviest brunt of attacks, whenever something new involving black people and their needs emerges. If a non-urban area government-sponsored housing project is specifically designed for lower-income families, this translates into "for the blacks," in the minds of many. And this leads to the unspoken but none the less fully understood: "We'll keep them out by any available legal or political means."

During the hearing on the New Hyde Park housing project—a hearing which took place almost concurrently with our own before the North Hempstead Town Board, local housing officials described the desperate need for the proposed housing.

Black families were living under near ghetto conditions in the Spiney Hill (Manhasset) area, paying high rents for slum quarters and unable to buy or rent anything better at any price. The housing officials pointed out, during another obstreperous hearing before the Town Board, that this was "one of the few remaining land parcels in the town suitable for low-income housing." It was bordered on three sides by major highways and on the remaining side by an office-industrial complex.

Many Negro families moving out of the gang-infested urban ghettos, to give themselves and their children a chance to live normal, decent lives, found that too often only the most inferior sub-standard housing was available to them in the suburbs. As the influx from the cities grew, the need for adequate housing increased, not only for non-white families but also for many lower-income and middle-income white families.

The housing authorities' proposal for this development was fully justified and needed. It was located in an area that could in no way be called a threat to the economic values of residential property in other sections of this community.

The land was zoned for low-density residential use. But then came the about-face, with residents and their supporters taking a wholly new tack. They proposed that the area be "downzoned" so it would not be used for housing projects or homes of any kind, but strictly and exclusively for business purposes. And yet, only a few short years before they heavily opposed this very use for an adjacent parcel.

As against the statement of town housing officials that this housing was essential to the community on the grounds of protecting residents, they insisted that they had "borne their burden" by approving a senior citizens' project and a town incinerator.

Some weeks later, when the Town Board voted four-to-one to kill the housing project for low-income families and allow a four-story office building to be erected on the property instead, and the decision was announced, the group who had been fighting against the housing project for low-income families broke into cheers.

Only one person on the board voted against this decision—made at the same time that the verdict on our own petition was handed down. He was the supervisor of the town of North Hempstead, and its Board Chairman, Robert C. Meade. It is an extraordinarily rare occurrence for a town supervisor to vote in direct opposition to his entire board.

Nor did Supervisor Meade hesitate to speak out at this meeting after the decision to tell the large gathering how unfortunate he considered this decision to be, in view of the critical housing shortage in the community. He announced that he would seek to draw community leaders together into a community housing committee that would begin to work with him and other leaders to deal with the problem. "Our talents and resources are most impressive when marshalled for a cause," he stated. "Now is not only the acceptable time, but possibly the only time."

When the verdict regarding this approval of down-zoning in New Hyde Park was announced, and the cheers of the "downzoners" swept through the hall, one woman wept. She was Mrs. Hazel Dukes of Roslyn Heights, Long Island, president of the NAACP representing a number of the townships in the immediate area.

"Blacks are being denied the right to live and walk freely in this town," she told the Board and the gathering. She said that black housing should not be built in poverty areas but should be located in districts where blacks and whites could live together.

A handful of others spoke in favor of Mrs. Dukes's position. She was quoted as declaring: "The fight is not over. We will still succeed."

There was no doubt that Supervisor Meade, a staunch Republican and conservative, had made a brave and forthright stand on an issue about which he knew there was need for sound and reasonable steps that morally should have been taken but for other reasons were rejected. At a meeting of business executives in the community, the North Hempstead supervisor described the hate mail and phone calls he received—a handful of angry individuals badgering him as a "nigger lover" and writing him letters of denunciation. One such letter was addressed to the "Not-so-honorable Judas Meade," in crude handlettering. Another letter writer expressed his fervent wish that the "curse of the Kennedy family" would fall upon him.

Meade described the extent of the fear that people in the area had on this subject of housing as unbelievable. "You can feel it, you can almost touch it," he told his listeners at this lunch of Long Island business executives. And the result he described as generating "a white, blurry atmosphere where reasoned discussion is impossible."

In the midst of all this turmoil, I wondered: Could I make any of this different? Could I change any minds or hearts by sitting down and talking with white militant or non-white militant? Can we force people to put aside prejudice or ignorance or hate? Of course not. And it doesn't matter whether you are talking about a black man or a legless man or a sightless man or even an old man.

I couldn't make the opposition see things in any different light. What am I—a pair of colored glasses to change their vision of the world?

Yet should you ask if I could change the *thinking* about disabled people: I believe I could. But I could do this only in degree, not in kind. And that is really the issue we have to face here. I could make them understand that disabled people can work, they are trainable, they can support themselves. But could I change their prejudice about having me as a husband for their daughter with my twisted stumps in artificial limbs? Could I change their prejudice against having a school for crippled children in the neighborhood? The answer is no. They would believe in the need, they would believe theoretically at least in the right of a legless man to marry somebody perhaps. But must it be their daughter? Must it be in their neighborhood?

This is their problem; it is still—even today—the problem of mankind.

Am I saying that what has happened to black and other ethnic and economically depressed peoples, and what happens to people like myself and Alex and hundreds of thousands of other disabled, is the same thing, that they are the same cause, that they must fight side by side, cause by cause? The answer has to be yes. For the wellsprings of all prejudice are the same: ignorance, superstition, fear, although the depth and shape and nature of the symptoms are different. Each cause is unique in some respects, identical in others.

I have the advantage over my black brother in one sense; he would not and indeed could not hide his face. But it is easy for me, you know. The sight of me when I wear my artificial limbs, standing in my academic robes, delivering a commencement address, may be, as some people have told me, really inspiring. Or if they could see me sailing my sloop off Port Washington, or working in my garden—it's all right. "There is that Dr. Viscardi, weeding in his garden, just like anybody else." But seeing me in a pair of swimming trunks sitting on the edge of the Human Resources pool is something else. I've a fine muscular body from the waist up. But it is quite different when you look at those malformed stumps I call my legs.

And some people are repelled by the sight of this, because deep within themselves they are afraid, because it might have been they, because it could be someone they loved. They don't think of how much happiness I have found in life—as do so many disabled persons—and how much I may have accomplished. But they think: What a dreadful thing to live with all your life. Would it have been better if he hadn't been born at all?

Or is it a matter of conformity? Is that what they require of us? Must we all look beautiful in a bikini, in accordance with the Hollywood ideal? Or must we be miserable, laughless, bitter, as some suspect most disabled people are? I know many miserable people who are disabled. But I also know as many or more who are not in the least bitter, and some of those with the most severe disabilities I have ever seen are among the happiest people I have ever known.

These are some of the things they say about us. But there are other things they say about the Blacks, Puerto Ricans, Mexicans, Italians, Jews, Catholics. What weapons or words are hurled depend upon what the hatred happens to be.

They want to tear us down, they want to halt our programs and progress for our people, they want us to take our children and go somewhere else, anywhere else. So we become the convenient symbol of the enemy; we become the mortgage payment, the Long Island Railroad when it's late in the sleet. If we weren't the issue, something else would be, because we aren't really their problem. Their problem is much deeper than this.

But now by force of circumstance, I am the symbol, the convenient symbol, the cause against which they do battle.

It is a curious thing, how two groups of our opposition in this area have subtly merged, intermingled, those individuals fighting low-cost housing on one side, those fighting against us on the other. It was nothing formalistic, but it was an affinity. They took the same approaches, the same attitudes, their lawyers and groups, even though the neighborhoods were some miles apart, were in a sense confederated.

Some of my friends wondered if I would not consider some kind of compromise in this struggle for our school. My answer to this is simply: How can you compromise the truth? Am I doing anything that isn't in the best interests of the community? It is either true or false, just or unjust; there are no gray areas. What compromise can you make with truth and justice?

I could make no compromise because I would not betray things which in conscience I believe to be right, ideas and goals I am sure the majority of our community itself supports. Most of the people are with us. Most support us enthusiastically and willingly. The hard, bitter core who make the loudest noises do not really represent the majority or the prevailing opinion of this community. If they did, then I could seek land elsewhere and go. But they do not represent the majority of people in the community.

Against all of this swirling emotionalism and its underlying reasons, there remains, however, the central issue: will they succeed in halting us, in preventing our work from going forward? The issue as this is written is not yet settled.

8

DATELINE:
WHERE YESTERDAY MEETS
TOMORROW

In the very midst of all that we were trying to cope with, I received word that I was expected shortly in Australia, a distance of ten thousand miles from our home, from my desk and my work for Human Resources.

It was an assignment, a solemn commitment I had made from which I could not turn. I had made a promise to a very wonderful rehabilitation leader, Lionel Watts, the severely disabled head of an Australian organization very similar to Abilities and Human Resources.

Watts was in the process of building a new facility for his work to be known as the House With No Steps. He needed funds to carry on this construction. But many Australian business leaders, like many in our own country in the past, were uncertain about what kind of role, if any, the handicapped could play in industry on a practical basis, and they were therefore understandably reluctant to put substantial sums of money into this kind of construction.

When Watts was in America many months earlier, we had talked about the problem.

It was at that time, listening to his needs and problems and realizing that his cause was mine also, even though it was halfway around the world, that I made the commitment from which I could not and would not back away at a later date.

Our relationships with Australian rehabilitation actually went back over a considerable period of time.

For some years we had been providing training for visiting Australian rehabilitation people at our Center in Albertson. Quite a few had come to Human Resources to study our methods. We had been pleased to discover that the Australian approach to the disabled was, like ours, largely unorthodox. They were, like us, ready to accept imaginative improvisations to solve an individual's problem; they were ready to take seeming risks that had held back human beings from even trying to expand their abilities. They, too, had heard again and again the old familiar: "But how could we let a child like that—without arms—play with other children? We wouldn't dare . . ."

But at Abilities, at the Human Resources School, on our playing fields, such children played, rough and tumble, our own rugged brand of soccer, hockey, football, or our own form of bowling or golf.

Like many of the Australians who came to see us and to study our ways, I did not hold with the textbook-haunted traditionalists who keep trying to tell us what can't be done and mustn't be done—but who so often cannot see or envision demands and needs that call not for negative but for affirmative creative response.

The fact is that I don't agree with the pampered approach or that of the ultra-conservative educational or medical people. I think one solves problems by grabbing them right by the neck and looking them right in the eye and getting them settled. Too often the psychiatrists only confuse the issue and make it almost impossible to do anything at all.

I am not in the camp of the orthodox in dealing with and solving problems of disability. Too frequently the best trained persons are still basically report-writers, protocol people, wheelspinners who too often substitute words and high-sounding phrases in place of getting things done that must be done. Some of them live in fear that they might violate the canons and rituals of textbooks. As one of my associates puts it, "They're afraid to take any step without checking on it first. If you say good morning, they say to one another, 'What did he mean?' "

The Australians, in any event, seemed to like our way better. We had begun to get letters from them over the last few years; they had started workshops built on the formula we developed at Abilities. They were fascinated also by the concept of our school for those who, by usual rules, were considered too handicapped for any regular school program.

Over these years, I had received a number of requests to go to Australia to lecture at some of the centers established there for the handicapped. Paralleling American statistics, they had, according to their best estimates, approximately one disabled individual for every six or seven non-disabled.

One late fall day my secretary announced that a lady and gentleman from Australia were waiting outside to see me. The man was Lionel Watts who was in a wheel chair and the very attractive lady with him was his wife, Dorothy.

This delightful couple came in to see me. He was quadriparetic, with little use of arms or legs. Once he had been normal. Now his wife was his arms, his legs and his guide.

We had a very fine chat as we toured our campus and explored its variety of workshop activities, its research laboratories, its classrooms and swimming pool and landscaped grounds. One of the things many who visit us comment on is how efficiently we operate our plant and campus, and yet how beautifully our buildings and grounds merge into the community around us.

Watts appeared astounded at what he saw, at how far we had progressed in our work activities, our research, our rehabilitation. As founder and director of the Wheelchair and Disabled Association of Australia, he was my counterpart in Sydney, working for and speaking on behalf of disabled people. "Hank, you're my kind of guy," he said at one point on our tour. "You cut through all the fuss and get things done."

"It isn't always easy," I reminded him. "A lot of people don't agree with our wide-open approach. But I think it is effective."

They were staying at the Waldorf. I asked them if they would care to have dinner with Lucile and me that night. I try not to surprise her too often with unexpected guests but if I call early enough there is always something in the pot for a guest or two, especially so far from home.

Lionel Watts had become quadriparetic as a result of a severe case of polio. He was not only married but had two children. And this wonderful woman, his wife, had been with him all these years, helping him. I found her to be like Lucile, truly a dedicated human being, with an overwhelming love for this man and for his work. Watts' accomplishments in Australia are comparable to mine in the States. We could not decide, in fact, whether I should be called the Watts of America or he the Viscardi of Australia.

I asked him how he had traveled to Abilities from the Waldorf Astoria Hotel on Manhattan's Park Avenue. Lionel said he hadn't known how far it was so he had taken a taxicab. That taxi fare must have run over twenty dollars.

At night during dinner at our house, we talked about the things human beings talk about, war, peace, nations and people, needs and problems. It was during this conversation that he said, "Hank, I need you in Australia. We need your inspiration and help. We haven't quite convinced all our government and business people that they have to be partners in this. Too much of it is still in the hands of the medical people and the therapists. We've got to get it off the ground with strong support from the private sector of our economy, which we haven't really had to date. You've got to promise to come—soon."

I caught the urgency in his tone. It was a call, a plea

for help, the kind we also have made, and still make, so many times in this difficult field of ours. I promised him that if he said that it had to be done, I would do it. Expenses would be paid by Australian rehabilitation agencies. Watts wanted us to stay for three months. I said three months was impossible. I said I could commit myself—if and when actually needed— to no more than three weeks. He agreed to this condition and my commitment was made.

When the call came that they really needed me there, I knew that it did not matter how our situation had changed in America, I could not back down on my word. There were others who could handle problems on the home front for those weeks in any case. There was always the transoceanic telephone to deal with an unlooked-for development.

Nevertheless, as I told Lucile, I was deeply concerned. This journey to tell Australian leaders about our work, our approaches and techniques and achievements, was important to them and to us. It was part of our job, and we were particularly happy to help such remarkable people as Lionel and Dorothy Watts. But I could not forget also, much as I would have liked to, that our own overwhelming problems still remained.

Lucile and I flew out on the Australian Qantas Airways with a brief stopover in California and on to Honolulu where we stayed overnight to rest and become acclimated to time-zone changes. While there we had a visit with two Chinese-American-Hawaiians, parents of Dr. Matthew Lee, a Johns Hopkins graduate who is a member of our medical advisory research team, serving both the Human Resources Center research program and the Abilities medical program. We had a Hawaiian dinner and a visit with the Lees in their lovely home on the outskirts of Honolulu. The next evening we left by Qantas plane again, flying across the evening twilight on to Nandi, and continuing on through the Pacific night after refueling. Dawn was breaking as we left Fiji. Five hours later we were landing at the airport in Sydney.

One ego-building episode occurred en route. On the plane I began reading an Australian publication called *Women's Weekly*. Leafing through it I came upon an article about myself, a full-page story that included a picture of my twenty-six-foot sloop and an account of how I sail it single-handed. Some weeks earlier a correspondent for the publication had come to Albertson to interview me and Lucile and the girls. Australians are sportsmen and sailors and they want to take "The America's Cup" away from us. But the story indicated considerable respect for a man with no legs who could handle a racing sloop like that alone. Finding that story in the publication, as I was about to arrive in Australia, seemed to me a good luck omen.

I had some minor difficulties clearing through the immigration people in Sydney, however; they are very fussy about disabled people immigrating to Australia. I probably would have had great difficulty if I had been applying for permanent citizenship, although my work in America might have helped open doors. But the immigration officer hadn't the least idea who I was and the moment he saw whom I was visiting—the Wheelchair and Paraplegic Association—he insisted that I had to fill out special forms.

This resulted in considerable delay. As an American citizen who respects his own inalienable rights, I did not appreciate the situation and said so firmly. I pointed out that I was not about to become a charge on the state, that I had come the guest of the association at their special invitation to talk to people throughout the country, that some of those people were meeting me here at the airport and that they were supposed to include a number of gentlemen of the Australian press, radio and television.

The official didn't retreat from his forms but instead of insisting that I fill out the numerous detailed questions—to indicate in general whether or not I was about to be selling pencils on Sydney's main street—he suggested that I simply sign the forms without bothering to read the details. I have no real idea what the forms said. The man said "Sign here" and I signed. When I asked some of my Australian colleagues what the immigration official and the form-signing were about they couldn't explain either. Whether in America or Australia, apparently the bureaucratic lines of itemization and differentiation remain.

Once they let me through the gates, however, I was startled at the contrast, the sudden warmth in the greeting Lucile and I received. We were taken into a large room where there were newsmen, TV cameras and a host of people from various organizations waiting to greet us. I was thankful that I had heeded my wife's advice to shave and spruce up on the flight in from Fiji.

Questions began with the usual direct approach—why had we come to Australia, what did I have to say to the Australian people about the disabled, what is it you do in your center in the United States that we don't do here? Did I think that Australia was ahead or behind America in dealing with the problem of rehabilitation?

Wisdom calls for caution in dealing with such questions in far-off cities or nations, whether it is Asia, Europe or Australia. You can't start by telling people all the things you think they are doing wrong. I explained that I had come not to teach so much as to learn. I was anxious to meet and talk with rehabilitation leaders in the country, to visit with many old colleagues who had been at our center. I said that any Australian sitting in Sydney with two artificial legs was no different from me, that he probably had the same hopes and aspirations and desires I did, to support himself, to love, to be loved, to seek his own destiny and not be a ward of the state or his family.

I put emphasis on the tremendous opportunities of their country—a nation as large as the United States with a population no greater than that of Long Island, where we live, a land of unlimited natural resources. I pointed out that the greatest natural resource of all were its human resources. I told them that my business dealt with trying to help human beings achieve a full life, even though they are disabled. I explained a little of the philosophy on which Abilities and Human Resources have been built: essentially, that our emphasis is not on what a man cannot do but what he can, not on the disability but on what abilities he has available to call on. "The amputee who sits in Sydney wants a life of dignity and self-worth just as I do, just as any other human being does. And he wants to support himself by his own efforts. This is the key."

These are simple concepts. They are concepts our work at Abilities has helped to spread widely across America and in other countries.

Some of the reporters seemed to find these ideas quite new and even revolutionary. After a number of other questions, they turned to Lucile, to find out what it was like being married to a legless man, and did my daughters have any feeling of aversion toward me because I was legless? And how did we meet and what did she do to help me? One of the reports in the Australian press quoted her as follows:

"I have never been bothered by the fact that my husband is handicapped.

"I suppose if I'd thought about it a lot I might have been concerned. But as it is, it has never worried me, so I've only been concerned with the success of my marriage and the happiness of my children.

"My work is in the home where I am kept busy entertaining Hank's business acquaintances and our friends.

"And I have four daughters to bring up."

That afternoon, after we were settled in a hotel, we were given a formal reception at the Governor's Palace where we met the Governor-General and pre-

sented him with some of the engraved glassware produced at Abilities. The journey of tours, speeches,
press conferences had begun.

Lionel Watts, who was with us on the tour, told me
he wanted to awaken wider business segments in the
Australian economy to the role the handicapped could
play in that economy.

I agreed to help in this; I wanted the trip to be
productive. I told him to keep me busy and on the go.
It was a hard-pressed and hard-pressing round of lectures, visits, tours, speeches at lunch and dinner, question-and-answer sessions day and night, TV and radio
appearances and interviews—a running journey with
hardly a moment to spare. Lionel Watts was with me
on most of the tours and provided valuable guidance
in my presentation of our concepts to Australian business leaders, and to the general public. Many of these
concepts, particularly relating to the role of severely
disabled persons in industry, presented ideas that few
business leaders had previously considered seriously.
This was no different from what I had been through
in our own country. In a land where actual shortages
of trained or trainable manpower exist, here was a
source of help that many of these leaders had not
before regarded as practical or workable. Yet the disabled could play an important role in this young, in-
novative, imaginative nation; they could provide
meaningful manpower and production.

I was deeply interested also in the rehabilitation
center Lionel and his group are in the process of constructing in Sydney—the one called the House With

No Steps. It too will play a major role in this re-education process.

Lionel and Dorothy Watts accompanied us on part of our trip. After we visited Adelaide, Lucile had to hurry home to the family. I continued on to Perth and then to Melbourne. There are a number of question-and-answer radio shows in Australia, with the public calling in on open phones as in America. Their concerns and attitudes appeared much like ours. The public there, as elsewhere, had a wealth of misinformation and erroneous concepts about disabled people, precisely as does our public in America. I could not help but reflect on the storm brewing with our neighbors, our new buildings, our school.

At one government building we visited, the only thing the group we spoke to wanted was to see my artificial limbs and how they were made. They had little interest in my philosophy, or what I represented; they were concerned about how I walked. Nothing else. I found myself a sort of specimen under a microscope. And while I was at first annoyed at this, I quickly got over that feeling because I realized that this, too, was important; it was, in effect, an achievement to let them see this, to let them begin to understand what can and is being done.

All the time I was in Australia, I kept hoping that I was making a contribution, a real contribution, by bringing them this first-person report on our methods, our approach, our achievements. I think it is valuable, this kind of missionary work in a nation so far from us. Perhaps I would never get to this country again. I wanted very much to do whatever I could in whatever time I had there. The long journey would be worthwhile if I could make the difference for only one disabled Australian, the difference between a life of productive dignity and one of dependency.

One of the ways of helping was to tell our story. In one address over the Australian Broadcasting Commission network, later reproduced in a magazine called *Progress*, the publication of the Australian Wheelchair and Disabled Association, I tried to sum up some of our own achievements in Albertson:

"In 17 years they (our working staff of disabled personnel in Abilities) have produced goods valued at $42,646,000. They have earned salaries of $21,904,000. They have paid taxes of $4,813,000. And we have invested in insurance, rehabilitation, benefit programs a total of $17,548,000.

"It would have cost $9,696,000 to have maintained them on relief rolls. If we add this cost to what they produced and earned and what was spent out of earnings for their benefit, the total of new wealth these so-called disabled have returned to the economy in 17 years is $96,607,000.

"Tell me what it produced in human dignity, personal happiness to them and their families. It is incalculable."

"This is a remarkable thing about our disabled people—in fact, about all people."

In Australia or America, this was the measure of the true statistics of our lives.

Grinning ear to ear, this young camper from Human Resources Center gets an autograph from the New York Mets during an outing at Shea Stadium.

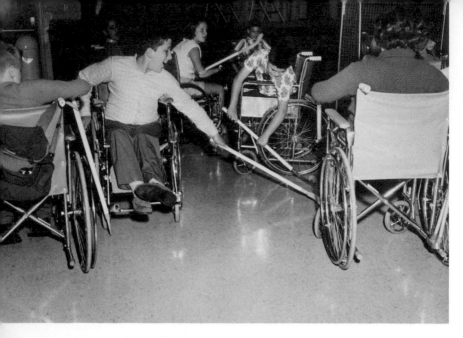

A full range of adapted sports is included in the curriculum of Human Resources School. All of the students enjoy participating in games such as football, soccer, and baseball—all of which have been modified to their special needs.

In order for the disabled young adult to become independent, he must be able to provide for his own transportation. The school offers driver education classes each summer for this purpose, in a car modified with hand controls.

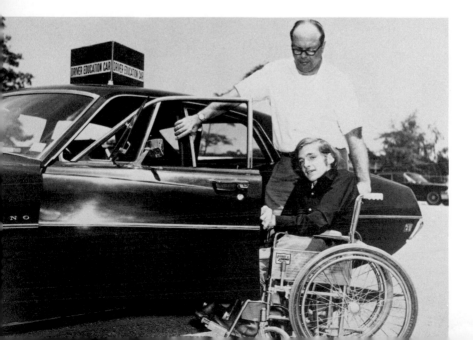

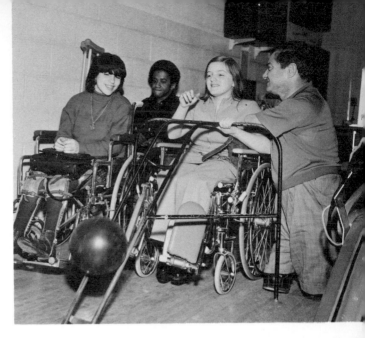

The specially modified bowling device allows even the more severely disabled youngster to know the joy of recreation. With the aid of a counselor, the disabled child can bowl with only the slightest movement of an arm.

Outdoor recreation facilities at Human Resources Center are all covered with either astro-turf or uni-turf surfacing materials which are easy to wheel across and which protect the disabled child in case of a fall.

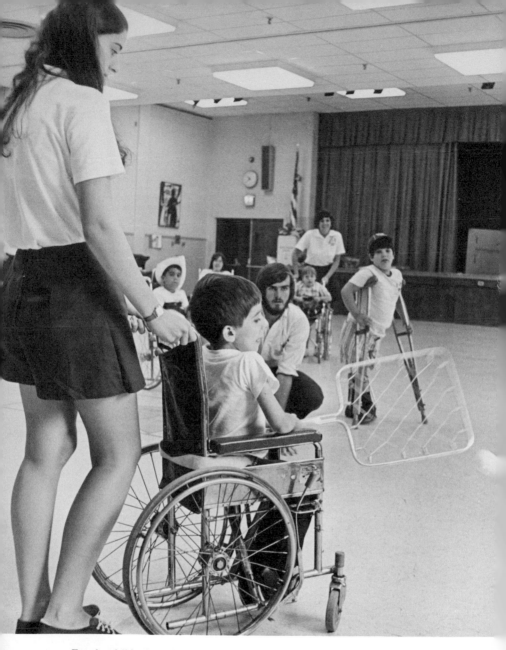

For the child whose disability has weakened his muscle control, unique apparatus must be designed if he is to partake in sports with his friends. Each of the modified sports of Human Resources School's recreation program is developed and evaluated so as to meet the requirements of such children.

I felt that the trip, the talks, the interviews, had served a real purpose, if only in awakening questions in the mind of the general public. At the same time, I had my own worries: the situations and developments we ourselves were facing at home. They were never far from my thoughts. I kept reflecting on what could be happening during this brief but important assignment in Australia.

The time that followed was crowded. But I was sorry Lucile could not share it with me. Way out in Western Australia, I visited a school of handicapped children. They were all out on the lawn looking out on the Indian Ocean. They were waiting for me. On my arrival, they sang a welcoming song. It was a very touching moment. I was thinking that their destiny was no different—should be no different—from that of my own children, who were perfectly whole, no different from that of any other children anywhere in the world, no different from that of all humanity.

The tour was hard. It was a running tour of interviews and talks and TV programs, from one hour to the next, exhilarating, exciting, tiring. But the drain on one's energies is always heavy. I found myself missing not only Lucile and the girls, but also our school and our campus. But still none of this wearing schedule diminished my excitement and interest in this Australian adventure in a new approach to disability.

When the tour was done, and I said goodbye to my charming hosts, the Wattses, and thanked them for this opportunity they had given me to make this journey to Australia, I started home. I flew straight through without any stopovers.

On the flight back, I tried to sort out in my own mind what we had seen there. It had been a two-way street of learning; I, too, had gained insights into their problems—and perhaps also our own. For we had seen the new suburbs of Australia, and discovered that they were not very different from similar communities in America. They had the same needs, desires, the same reasons for existing and growing, even some of the same problem situations. I would guess that they shared some of the same prejudices and thinking, in a greater or less degree.

We were all people, all the same, not different, with varying degrees of weakness and strength.

Flying through the night, across the Pacific Ocean, heading homeward where by now I longed to be, I realized that I could not hate those who think about the disabled in primitive terms. I say these are latent feelings that they rarely allow to surface in any form. Yet those of us who live it know what they really think. How could a girl like Lucile, they ask, intelligent, attractive, marry a man without legs, and then have four children by him? How could they truly love without there being a sense of regulation?

These are their questions, their ideas.

I was thinking also of that Dorothy Watts whose husband had lost all motion in his legs and most of the motion in both arms and hands, of how they were a happy couple in their lives and work and travels, and in their love and concern for each other.

It is easy to grow angry at injustice, at the brutal assaults man so often makes upon his fellow man, especially upon those who are different from the norm, whatever it may be. There are no boundaries in this kind of aggression. It races across nations, oceans, continents, centuries. What I was winging my way home to was no different from what was to be found elsewhere, no different from the mélange of erroneous information that has always divided our world into sheep and goats, the blessed and the damned, the able and the disabled.

I was convinced, too, that it was no different two thousand years ago; it is clear that hate and rejection of that age was very much the same as now. It culminated in a crucifixion and centuries later in what happened in Germany to the Jews was another kind of crucifixion. We kill and suffer and seek forgiveness.

All of this was running through my mind.

The fine work of the people in Australia with the disabled could not be questioned. Yet still they had their needs, their problems, their desires, their frustrations. Perhaps what I took back was this identity of need and understanding and compassion.

We stopped briefly enroute at the Island of Fiji and at Honolulu for an hour. In Honolulu I walked around the airport and bought some shaving cream. In California we had a two-hour layover.

I insisted on going to a hotel. I had a hot bath, which helped my stumps, and shaved. I had a cocktail and dinner and I called Lucile and told her how much I loved her and that I was on my way home.

Six hours later I was back at our home in Great Neck. Lucile was waiting with a warm embrace and a smothering of welcome-home kisses.

9

NINA

||||||||||||||||||||||||||||||

Coming home like this, after that whirlwind ten thousand miles, made me acutely aware of two things: the importance of my work on the one hand, on the other, the importance of my personal life, my family, my wife and daughters.

A man's life, handicapped or otherwise, is measured in the areas of both his work and his personal life. The one does not hold meaning, cannot exist without the other. When I come home it is without fear of offending anyone because I am legless. After dinner, in robe and pajamas, when I take off my artificial limbs, I ride around in my wheel chair and relax—and one of the girls may push me, out of her love for me.

How hard it is for our friends and neighbors to grasp this simple reality! How hard it is to explain to them that I am not a legless man to my family but the father of four beautiful girls—a man, a husband, a father, a human being.

I remember how Nina, my oldest daughter, went away, the first one to leave, to attend the College of Notre Dame in Baltimore. By the time she came back for the first holiday she was beginning to be grownup, full of new ideas she was hearing and discussing. I recall Lucile saying: "You'll have to talk to her, Hank. She's in another world."

Of course she was. During these years she was going through a dozen phases with all her plans for what she wanted to do and be; she was a trailblazer, as the oldest of the four girls, all of whom ultimately would go to college. Nina spent one summer as a fellowship student at Dr. Howard A. Rusk's Institute of Physical Medicine and Rehabilitation. She worked there with crippled children and became so excited over this activity she wanted to leave her regular college work and switch to a school of occupational therapy. Switching schools like that was not easy in mid-August. Ultimately it did not work out and she returned to Baltimore. Two weeks after she arrived at the college there she called us to tell us, "You'll be happy to know I'm now an art major."

She was obviously excited about this new field, although we never knew she had any talent whatever in that area or could even draw a straight line. A few days later Nina cut a large incision in her thumb with a sculptor's chisel and had to have a few sutures to close the gash. That was more like it, I told Lucile. No doubt about it, this was our gal. Any day, I warned, we would hear she was allergic to the paints.

But no mind. We were delighted for her and we were inundated with enthusiastic correspondence about her studies. She was getting high marks and was in the top third of the class with A's and B's in all her courses. I insisted only—with all my daughters—that they become certified to teach. I didn't care whether they taught or not; I thought of it as a kind of insurance. With Nina, it paid important dividends.

By her senior year, we were hearing a lot about Brian Sharkey, a senior at Villanova. All of us liked Brian, an engineering student in the Navy ROTC program. Nina finally came to us and said they were really serious about marriage and wanted to become engaged. Lucile and I agreed this was wonderful and I said we'd be glad to talk to Brian. Nina said, "Could he at least talk to you alone, Dad, instead of making it a family conference?"

"Sure," I said. "Let's not make this a big deal. I mean, he really doesn't have to get all uptight about it."

And Nina said, "I'd like to marry Brian after I am graduated and then get a place to live and teach in Philadelphia while Brian finishes his engineering course."

I wasn't so sure that this was the right approach. Fathers always think they know best. But I told her I'd talk with him.

Brian did come to see me before the graduation in June, and I must say I never saw a more nervous boy. I said, "Brian, why don't you relax?"

Brian said, "I find it difficult."

I said, "You know, you and Nina could run off to Elkton, Maryland, which isn't far from Baltimore, and get married and send us a telegram. And what could we do about that?"

Brian looked shocked at what I thought was mildly humorous. "Oh," he said. "I would never do a thing like that, not to you, not to Mrs. Viscardi or to Nina. I love her too much. But we do want to get married. I think I would make a good husband for her."

He went on to explain that the engineering course took five years and they wanted to get married before the fifth year began and move down to Philadelphia. "You'll have it tough," I warned.

But he said, "No. Nina graduates in June. If she gets a job teaching, and she's certified now, I think we can just squeak by."

What a strange, wonderful situation I found myself in, as a father talking to a prospective son-in-law. I could not help but remember how very much I loved Lucile and wanted her to be my wife, and how fearful I had been that perhaps she or her family would not want me. And now one of the lovely girls she had given me was being asked for by a young man. It was a long road for a crippled boy to have travelled.

"Brian," I said, "you know, in my own life, I never dreamed I'd ever meet a lovely girl like Lucile and marry her. All those years as a crippled child, most of my early years in a hospital, and finally painfully growing up in that Upper West Side jungle on my deformed limbs. Then college and the world of books. Remember, I didn't stand on artificial limbs until I was twenty-seven years old.

"But as I grew into adolescence I also was a young man with dreams and desires. I wrote poetry and dreamed of how wonderful it would be if someone

would love me, would be my wife. But I didn't think
that could ever be because I was a cripple. I stood then,
without artificial limbs, three feet, eight inches high.

"Now I think of all the wonderful things that have
happened since that time: the wonderful woman I
married, our wonderful daughters. But among the
things I would never have dared to dream would be
that one day some young man like you would come
and ask for my daughter's hand in marriage. It's a
significant thing for me. It has overtones that I hope
you will understand. And I want all of us to have the
best of all of this, on the best possible terms."

I paused. There was a little silence between us.
"That's why I would hope," I went on finally, "that
you wouldn't get married in June and go through all
that time of struggle while you're getting your degree.
Why not put it off a little time, until you have finished
with your studies and are ready. Nina could live at
home. She has been away from us for four years at
college. We would love to have her for these last
months."

We discussed it a little more then, and I talked later
with Nina and Lucile about this. It was decided—as I
should have known, for all my grandiose remember-
ing—that the date had to be left up to Brian and Nina,
after all. And Nina said, with all the confidence of the
young, "We have decided to be married at Christmas."

I know when a father has done his best and lost. I
told them Christmas would be great. Now I could
prepare to be the least important of men at the wedding, the father of the bride.

So we had a Christmas wedding, held in the chapel of the Merchant Marine Academy which is right next door to us, on the same grounds where Nina had lived since she was born.

And a little later, my second oldest daughter, Donna, came to me with a fine young man—and announced that they, too, planned to be married. So all the planning had to begin anew. And soon it would be the other girls as well.

We live in a world of the personal, all of us—Lucile, myself, the girls. Even Nina's cat.

The cat story actually began somewhat earlier, at the time Nina was graduated from Notre Dame. The family had flown down to attend the graduation but Nina and Brian (as yet unmarried) decided to drive home in our large station wagon with all the gear a girl accumulates in four years of college.

When they arrived home they had with them this scrawny little cat—a gray alley cat. It had been on her campus but now everyone was gone and the Sisters couldn't take care of it and here it was. A kitten that nobody wanted, and Nina wanted to know if we couldn't keep the poor little kitten overnight. Brian stayed out of it, hoping for the best.

Of course we had one ancient cat and one dog already but never mind that; we agreed that it could stay overnight. That was the least we could do. And, of course, everybody fed the cat and gave it something to sleep on. I never saw a cat respond with more affection than this diminutive character. He loved everyone, even the dog. He stayed over the next day and the next and, as wisdom might have anticipated, it was finally agreed we would have to keep the cat.

That was only the beginning. The cat had shots, and turned out to be not a he but a she. We took her back to the veterinarian to be spayed. "She can't be spayed," the vet informed us on the second visit. "She's pregnant." What's more she was allergic to the shots and had to be hospitalized to save her life.

Some college career this cat had. Nobody knew how or where it happened, but there it was. We changed her name from Tom to Mimi. The kittens were stillborn. After that she was spayed but something was wrong. Male cats howled outside our house all night long. Back to the vet for a total replay. That one took. Mimi is now a loveable lady cat with no more problems. She has settled down to a life of quiet domesticity and I estimated I have paid the vet enough to send his son through one semester of veterinarian school.

We wonder, though, if our domesticated feline doesn't sometimes dream of her extra-curricular college activities. I would appreciate it, in fact, if the College of Notre Dame could give me an indication of the curriculum content of the courses Mimi took while she was still on campus.

10

POLITICS AND PEOPLE

Politics and kittens perhaps have little in common
—not even with kittens like Mimi. But somehow she
was a symbol, to all of us in the family, despite her
checkered past—a symbol of laughter and love, in a
very warm personal sense. She and all our pets were
part of the magic private circle of our lives.

Politics was quite the opposite. It was the outside
world beyond the circle, the world in which I would
have to play a part on a new stage, a world not of one
minority but of many, each with his pressing needs
and demands.

Where did I belong in this picture? This was the
issue on which I personally had to reach a decision. It
was also the reason for an enlightening dinner at a
place called the Steak House.

The Steak House is a fine restaurant with private
rooms for business meetings. It is located half a mile
or so from Human Resources Center. Here, in one of
those private rooms, I had a meeting with some close
personal friends to seek their advice. It was time to
begin reaching final decisions that could no longer be

put off. Unlike my first consultation with my own people, this was a meeting with leaders from the outside.

In the midst of the Christmas season I had called Leonard Hall, who is one of the three influential leaders in the Republican Party."Len," I said, "I told you once I'd give you a chance to twist my arm about my running for Congress. This is it. Will you come to dinner with me in a private dining room with three or four of your peers and maybe tell me why I should become a congressman?"

A long pause. Then Len said: "Whom am I meeting with, Hank?"

"One is Otz Tracy. Official Name: O.T. Tracy."

An Annapolis graduate who after one career with Esso started a new career with the W.R. Grace Company, Otz is one of my close friends. He became vice-president of W.R. Grace from which he retired but still acts as consultant. When we were considering a plastic operation at Abilities, it was Otz who came out at Peter Grace's request to help us with the basic concepts and technology. It was a venture we decided was not for us. He has become a warm, dear friend.

I told him: "Otz will be there. Also Jack Retalliata, vice president of Grumman Industries. And Paul Townsend, editor of the Long Island Commercial Review. And Harold Gleason, president of Franklin National Bank." (He is now board chairman.)

"Great," Hall said. "I'll be delighted to have one of those backroom conversations with a gang like that and I hope it winds up with you agreeing to run, because I hear if you do run, you'll be elected."

That was from the man who was Eisenhower's campaign manager and former chairman of the Republican Party. I considered it a fairly reliable straw in the winds. If this was the way I wanted the winds to blow.

In any case, we met in a delightful room at the Steak House, a reasonable facsimile of a smoke-filled room, I suppose, to discuss the situation. We had a drink and dinner and I said, "Gentlemen, I realize I have to make up my mind. I'm not asking you to decide for me. But I am asking your guidance as close friends concerning what you would do in my position. I have to ask you to bear in mind that disability has been my life's cause, and I've enjoyed every minute of my activity in this field."

I explained to these men that while I had not sought the Congressional job, I was certainly drawn to it. "Quite frankly," I admitted, "the excitement and challenge of a new career interests me. But beyond that is the fact that I hate to hurt anyone I've tried to help, to hurt the cause that I've served. That would destroy me."

Once before in my life I had left the cause of the disabled to work at a high executive level in industry, only to be drawn back some years later by the needs of this cause.

Was it time now to seek a second career as a legislator? The excitement of a campaign, the national prominence if elected, were not to be denied. But could I leave my people—or, hopefully, serve them better, as a congressman?

As at the CIT luncheon, I wanted their opinions, suggestions, objective considerations of both sides. But now I had gone over this in my own thinking. Now, I needed truly definitive answers. Around the table were not only my close friends but the man who in addition to being my long-time friend was one of the two or three most knowledgeable politicians in America—Len Hall! His answers were professional as well as personal. And Len insisted with dogmatic certainty that I had to run. "Don't you see what you could do for Abilities people as a member of the Congress?" he demanded. "Any committee with a problem affecting disability would seek you out. The things you did to get elevators in Washington subways, as a member of the transportation group of the President's Committee, are nothing compared to what you could do for airlines, for buses, for automobile manufacturers, for job preference, for hospitals, for health. You can't turn your back on this, Hank."

Both politically and factually, this was a strong, persuasive statement. They wanted me nominated. They thought I could win.

Sitting beside Len Hall was Harold Gleason, president of Franklin National Bank. He announced that he had come to the meeting prepared to tell me that I shouldn't change from one career to the other at this critical point but went on to add that Len Hall's impressive statement had given him doubts. Reluctantly, "I think you should do it," he stated. "I think you could do more down there than you can up here to help."

He also explored the varied ways in which I could contribute, as a spokesman for the disabled, pointing out that I would not be merely another congressman nor merely a disabled congressman per se. There have been a number of disabled congressmen over the years, he said. I would be a spokesman, rather than an individual; I would be a symbol of disabled people. And I would be doing this on a stage as wide as in the nation and the world. Even far-off peoples who still might retain primitive cultures and equally primitive ideas about the handicapped might be reached.

Perhaps as nothing in history, he said, this position I would have could uplift the disabled, eliminate so much of the superstition that persists.

Listening to this bank president outline his thinking clearly and casually, I began myself to feel that it had the elements of truth, despite all my doubts. The Washington scene had this dramatic aspect: it was a platform on the public stage from which I could truly reach the world.

People in this kind of gathering are curiously put on their mettle to be frank, forthright in their opinions. Len Hall was putting it as he saw it, as was Gleason. Otz Tracy was equally forthright—but in the opposite direction. He declared as his opinion that under no circumstances should I run for the Congress of the United States.

"A man of your honesty, with your integrity, with your high principles, would be destroyed in the race for Congress and afterward if you were elected," Otz said. "Why, some of those people would chew you up

and you wouldn't even know you were being eaten
until you were gone. Worst thing you could do. You'd
be throwing your life away to go to Congress. We need
you right here."

These were strong words also, directly con-
tradicting the words of those two loyal friends.
And I understood that he was thinking of political
factions, liberal wings versus conservative, close
infighting, trading, tactics, ploy and counter-ploy
on the political scene. As my good friend Otz was
speaking I recalled Will Rogers once saying that every now and then an innocent man is sent to the
Congress.

But Otz was saying, "Hank, it is not your role.
You have another job to do."

The effect of his words in our not-too-smoke-
filled Steak House room was evident—the weight
and impact. In the luncheon at CIT I had sought
preliminary guidance, a beginning of forming an
important decision. But here, under somewhat different circumstances, with a firm commitment or rejection now obviously required within a very short
time, the opinions were more definitive.

I could not have two roles. It could not be
merely an addition to my present activities. It was
not a commuting operation. It would be giving up
the past. It would mean becoming a new being, a
political being, with all the ramifications of that
hard glittering designation. The local political advi-
sors had said I could hold down both jobs, as Human Resources Center President and as Congress-

man. Len Hall doubted this. It was always clear that I would resign my present job if elected to Congress.

Jack Retalliata, the industrialist and businessman, was himself caught in the dilemma of the situation. "When I came here," he told the group around the table, "I was convinced Hank should do this. I feel strongly that a man of his character should be representing one of our districts in Congress. I felt good that you would be speaking for things Long Island needs."

There was a silence around the table. Finally he went on, "But I've changed my thinking. As I listened to all this, I just don't believe you should do this, and I am going to recommend against it. We need you here and your voice here is being heard across the land and around the world."

Paul Townsend, the Commercial Review editor, announced that he likewise had changed his opinion, after listening to the discussion. "I came prepared to urge Hank to go," he said. "Now I'm not sure. In fact, I don't think he should. I'm an editor. I write a newspaper. I'd love to think of you down there, Hank, fighting like a tiger for things you believe in. But then I think—maybe you would be able to accomplish what you want or maybe nothing. What's more, I'm not sure you aren't needed right here. The job is far from done."

To me this was the most telling argument. The issue was not what I wanted to do but whether I should do, what I had to do.

I faced the question of whether I could or could not

properly leave the school in the uncertain situation it was in at that moment, with the whole building program at stake in the hearings that lay ahead. Or could I leave Abilities in its present economic situation which had forced us to drop from four hundred workers to less than two hundred and fifty.

Our losses for the year in Abilities were running about three-quarters of a million dollars. I was certain Abilities would survive but I was equally certain I had to remain on the scene, close to the situation, to provide leadership that would insure a successful turnaround.

Human Resources Center and our Research and Training projects were also facing challenges because of the recession situation. If I turned my back on these activities and went to Washington, it could be the beginning of the end of something I believed in deeply —something I had spent the last twenty years in building. This was the deep reality in my mind that night.

We talked until after eleven o'clock on a variety of subjects. But of course in the back of my thoughts was this major issue on which they had been so sharply divided in opinion, three to two, although as I indicated to them, I had decided to make the decision myself based on my best judgment.

That was the evening of December 19th. Everybody, especially wives and families, was deeply involved in Christmas preparations. I assumed everything would have to wait until after the holiday season was over. But I was wrong. On December 22, I had a

call from Bill Casey. He said, "You better come see
me, or I better come see you. You can't turn this down,
Hank. I've been to Washington again. I'm increasing
the pressure."

The urgency in his tone was obvious. They wanted
a decision. I said: "Bill, let's meet." So he had lunch
with me, at the Metropolitan Club in New York. I
gave him once more the basic points around which my
doubts and questions were shaped. The responsibilities of my life, both personally and in my work. And
whether I should uproot all of this at that critical
moment.

Bill was not about to let it go, however. He said I
could get assistants to take over much of the work. He
said he could get me substantial help on financing my
campaign; possibly he could even get Len Hall to manage the campaign. "I know the political scene," he told
me. "This is the kind of offer that comes only once in
a man's lifetime."

I agreed with all of this and was deeply affected by
his confidence in me and told him so. I said I would
love to do it. I said I'd let him know.

That night I talked it over with Lucile. This was
perhaps the most important part. We had talked about
it before and always in her wonderful way she had
said to think about it and pray over it and whatever I
decided she would agree to. I don't believe a man
should surrender his home or family to his work. I was
not going to do so in this instance. My wife and children were not to be brushed aside for my career.

Lucile was her usual frank and wholly honest self.

"Look," she said, "we've done a lot of wonderful things together. And if this is what you want, just count me in. I'll understand and we'll manage."

She could not, she said, give me an enthusiastic vote for it; she did not feel that way about it. "But you know where we stand, I and the girls. Right by your side. If Washington is where you want to go, we go together. Whatever you do, don't destroy yourself. We need you, Hank. Just be sure you want it."

We could not give up our home on Long Island. Nina was married. Donna and Lydia were away at college, but our youngest was happy in high school at St. Mary's. And Nana, Lucile's mother, was with us. This was our home. I would commute to Washington as a congressman.

I stood listening to Lucile's words, so quick, so sure, so unafraid, and I knew my answer.

The problem throughout this whole period was that they did not believe I meant it. I wrote Senator Caemmerer a letter to this effect just before Christmas, 1969, but he not only did not believe it, he called me two days before Christmas and asked me to meet with him at Republican headquarters. There I met a lot of important leaders in the community.

Considerable pressure at the gathering was brought to change my mind. One gentleman who was a local councilman cried out, "You're a winnah! You're a winnah! Boy, with your name, I can't miss, we can't miss carrying you into office. Everybody knows you, everybody loves you. What a candidate! You're gonna run. I hope you're gonna run."

And I thought, you know, it would be fun relating
to this exciting, rough-and-rugged kind of activity and
campaigning. It took me back to days long past when
I handled setting up radio broadcasts at the fights every Friday at Madison Square Garden and every Monday at St. Nicholas Arena. That was one of my early
jobs—with the Mutual Broadcasting system. All my
life, from my earliest days on New York's Upper West
Side, I relished that kind of challenge.

Senator Caemmerer said he'd received my letter,
didn't understand, and wouldn't accept it because he
could not allow me to throw away a golden chance like
this to be a congressman.

I thanked him and said the answer stands. He reiterated that he was hopeful I would reconsider. I said,
"John, it's the final answer. It's no."

It wasn't, of course, the final answer, because the
pressures did keep up, from many sides, all of them
enticing and insistent.

At the same time I was dealing with half a dozen
other critical issues. Many of these had to do with
economic and business problems at Abilities. The cut-
back in industry as the Seventies dawned affected us
too at Abilities. Many major companies for whom we
had taken on workloads were themselves hurt and
retreating. Contracts were hard to come by. There
was increasing unemployment. Small companies were
closing down. Long Island was an economic disaster
area. Planning for the future was reaching a critical
situation.

In addition to all of this, the organized activity and

antagonism against us from the immediate suburban world that surrounds us continued. There were more and more neighborhood meetings, plans and campaigns against us, and many of us felt that some of these people were determined to destroy us, to hound us out of there.

It was really difficult at times in the midst of all these pressures to see the course ahead to safe harbor.

It is even more difficult to leave a job for a bigger one at a time when you are most needed.

11

CRISIS

||||||||||||||||||||||||||||||||

In the late fall and early winter of 1970, our nation faced a crisis not only in Viet Nam but in terms of *all* human beings, handicapped or otherwise—the hard reality of inflation and recession and the grim meaning of layoffs for able and disabled alike.

For more than five years previous to that time our center had conducted a carefully planned program for developing our special skills and know-how, men and women who could sit for hours at full efficiency working on minute circuit systems and retrofit work on modern electronic components. We were deliberately building knowledge and expertise in servicing equipment of all types used by major manufacturing companies, particularly in the aircraft field. We spent many thousands of dollars in developing this new approach to our skills and economic opportunities.

We had gone far in establishing ourselves as a unique group of specialists in high quality precision work in important areas of "keeping the machinery flying." The large companies which built the original systems preferred not to retrofit them and we could do

132

such overhauling and rebuilding at less cost to the customer. Again and again, we demonstrated the ability to service equipment more efficiently than could major industrial plants. But even as we were developing this service concept we also began to feel the economic bind. It was no overnight thing, but rather a long slow retreat. Like hundreds, even thousands, of other companies, we had begun to complete various jobs only to discover that new contracts we had counted on were not coming in.

There had been hard times before, but what began in the Seventies ran deeper. This was a tide of economic change that had taken over and there appeared to be no way to reverse it quickly. There was no sudden crash, no headlines about a plunging stock market. Rather, it was a long slow slide of employment and production. The Long Island area with its heavy emphasis on military manufacturing was particularly hard hit just as it had been after the Korean War. This was a recession and all production, both military and commercial, was in trouble.

Jobs were not there. Orders were not there. Machinery in the shop ground to a halt. Our rows of workbenches were manned now by only a portion of the people who had once been there. We were still working at some new orders and contracts, and we had great hopes for the future—reasonable hopes, realistic plans. But we could not force the times; we were caught in the midst of a sudden national, even worldwide, economic storm.

Other companies, old-time companies, were cutting

back. But we had a situation to deal with different from those of other companies. There was literally *no* other place for most of our people to go. Even though many disabled workers compete on even terms or better with the non-disabled; many firms consider employing such workers to be a luxury that has to stop the moment things tighten up. Depression and recession are traumatic experiences for our workers; it runs through the entire organization—the insecurity, the not knowing whether or not we're going to have new work coming out on the floor when we're finished with this. Our workers can't just walk out and go elsewhere for a job.

Because of this special importance of the job to the disabled, because getting some other job outside could be impossible, our goal has always been to increase the stability of the product, the work load, to develop special skills into an on-going accepted phase of major industry, and to diversify, so that contracts would not wind down to none at all. This had been much of the fundamental thinking and motivation behind our decision to make Abilities a leading specialist, particularly in the banking and computer fields, in building and servicing electronic and other complicated, high-precision equipment.

Image for us was an important factor. Much of the business community still didn't understand Abilities. Even as the 1970 recession began to dig in, we were still working on a program to inform the data processing field more realistically as to our capabilities. We wanted them to know that we have competency here,

that we're not just a bunch of helpless cripples looking
for a handout, that we have the staff, the training, and
a computer capacity that can get the job done with
more precision and expertise than any other service
they could buy. After a great deal of research and
experiments we knew that our disabled people could
perform best in the areas of data preparation and analysis. These were the areas in which special skills were
needed that we could supply.

It's a rugged period when you go through the recession mill. Rumors start to fly, everyone knows something, everyone is frightened, uncertain. You catch
the hint of panic in the air. A rumor starts that Abilities will close for one solid month. People wonder if
there will be any jobs at all for anyone. With one hand
you fight for new workloads; with the other you are
trying to add up how many people you can keep on
another week. Each person has his special needs, his
problems. Each looks to you to help in such moments.

With this kind of thing developing, action had to be
taken. It was like a ship in a sudden heavy sea. Everyone had to be told, the word was spread that the rumors were untrue. We were not about to close. We
were in troubled times, but we had been there before
and weathered the storm and we would again. To me,
our people, the people of Abilities, are an integral part
of our entire operation, without whom we would be
nowhere, we would have no purpose, for the whole
demonstration at the adult working level would otherwise be lost.

It was in spite of, rather than because of, all this that

we forged ahead with our banking and data program, our analysis of markets and demonstrations for prospective customers, of investment in engineering capability so as to offer a complete service to a prospective customer. All of this was carried on out of our reserve funds, in the midst of other difficulties, as the economy shrank and orders from the major companies slowed almost to nothing. These were the funds we had set aside in the good years of Abilities' operations so that we could survive and make a turnaround in bad times.

And still we struggled on. We investigated new markets, new customers, engineered new areas of skills, fighting a desperate battle to reorganize activities and operations, including our glass engraving and our packaging operations, in both of which orders fell off dramatically in the first months of the economic slide.

At this time—because we can never underestimate the importance of the school—we were continuing to raise funds and fighting the community battle so that we could use these funds for the new building.

It was a time of uncertainties, of inconsistencies. On the one hand I supported the position of the operating head of Abilities, that we should continue to try to expand the role of Abilities despite all the difficulties, and even though we were losing money and having to dip into reserves to regroup our capacities to stay afloat. At the same time I was being pressed to run for Congress, which could mean that I would be leaving the whole scene were I to accept and be elected. In addition, I was working with the board and others in reorganization of our three structures and in bringing some of our people up to vice-presidential authority.

In the midst of all this confused alarm, the question in my mind resolved itself to its elemental meaning: Should we be worried that we were scurrying around in meaningless circles like frightened mice? Or were we proving, as we had done a number of times in our past, that we believed, even in such dark moments, in ourselves, in our destiny as disabled, and in our future?

It is not always easy to go on believing in the dream. So much, so many things close in. We have to believe in an equality that often doesn't work out, not in hard times at least.

My friend Alex, who has worked with me for so many years and about whom I have written in other books, talked with me about this too, in the midst of our struggle to build a gym and cafeteria for our youngsters. Alex, who has no arms and legs, who stands three feet six and who has been a member of our working force here for more than a decade, happens to be a Sephardic Jew. And he said to me, "Hank, you know, my own people, my own race, we're a minority. And yet, my people are against other minorities too. They're prejudiced against disability also. They don't want to look at me and my toothpick six-inch arms. They turn away . . ."

I knew what he meant. Minorities of all kind, however deeply they themselves feel the sting, are often inclined to forget the prejudice they have within themselves for other causes. I told Alex, "I don't think

it matters that some who object to me may happen to
be Irish or Jewish or whatever. Some of them, whatever they are, are for us, and some in opposition. What
difference does it make who it is? Isn't it the same
thing? There is a common denominator about disability. The sameness of being different and unwanted, I
have seen all over the world, in many cultures and
races."

"I wanted to mention it to you," Alex said. "Being
born a Jew and living as a Jew and also being all my
life a disabled person, I remember knowing from my
own boyhood that I was rejected by my own community. I wasn't invited to Bar Mitzvahs. I was excluded
almost on a religious basis."

I told him, "Alex, that's only because you happened
to live in that particular community. If you'd lived in
an Irish community, I'm sure the rejection would have
been the same. Or in an Italian community, a black
community, or a Greek or Asian."

I knew that what Alex was saying was at the very
heart of all prejudice, nonetheless. For he was talking
not about what people mean but about what they do
and say almost without knowing, without realizing
what they have done.

Let me cite a personal example of this. There have
been times when because of too much running around
my stumps have become inflamed. Then I must take
off the artificial limbs and for a brief period travel in
a wheel chair.

I travel all over the world on my artificial limbs. On
rare occasions, in an airport or railroad station or at

some other public place, if Lucile is with me, I may ride in my wheel chair and let Lucile push me.

But a strange thing happens then. When we reach a ticket window, the man or woman behind the counter usually does not speak to me. Suddenly, because I am in that chair, I cease to exist as an entity, a human being. With me sitting right there beside my wife, the ticket agent will say to her, "Now what is his name? Where is he going? How much luggage does he have?"

This curious syndrome happens regularly to anyone who is in a wheel chair that is being pushed by someone else. The individual in the chair is treated by clerks or policemen or strangers or whoever it may be as though that individual either doesn't exist at all, or as if he is deaf and dumb, or simply imbecilic. It doesn't always happen this way but it is too constant a pattern to be ignored. What causes it, fear, revulsion, sympathy, ignorance, I do not know. It is one small gnawing sample of the mindless aberrations of prejudice.

On the walls of my office at Human Resources I have more than a dozen honorary degrees and citations from leading universities both here and abroad. Yet I have endured this experience countless times.

When John Gardner was Secretary of Health, Education and Welfare, I did a series of programs on rehabilitation for the National Broadcasting Company, in the course of which I interviewed the HEW Secretary twice. I found him to be truly a tremendous human being. The things that he has written, his thoughts and observations on the present scene and its problems are to me so fundamentally American; his ideas point a road to the future, to awareness, to understanding not only of ourselves but perhaps—hopefully—those around us.

I recall talking to him, during one period in our early struggles, about the tactics we encountered, the denunciations, the vituperation, the assaults on our motives, even our integrity. I recall this comment at that time: "Sad to say, Hank, a good many people find it fun to hate."

That is the trouble—too many find it fun. Rage and hate in a good cause are the fashion. It is, as Gardner put it, always in a good cause. Be vicious for virtue, self-indulgent for higher purpose, dishonest in the service of a higher honesty. Too often that is philosophy.

This was the crisis we faced. A crisis of ourselves, our work, our role.

It was a crisis also of prices, of rising costs, of depression and recession. It was the crisis of all those around us to whom we were the enemy, the crippled whom they professed to love. But was it perhaps as the segregationist loves his black neighbor?

It was a crisis of all these things, economic, political, social. A cauldron of civic turmoil, of cities and suburbs, of riot in the streets and in the high temples of governments and courts and meetings in town halls.

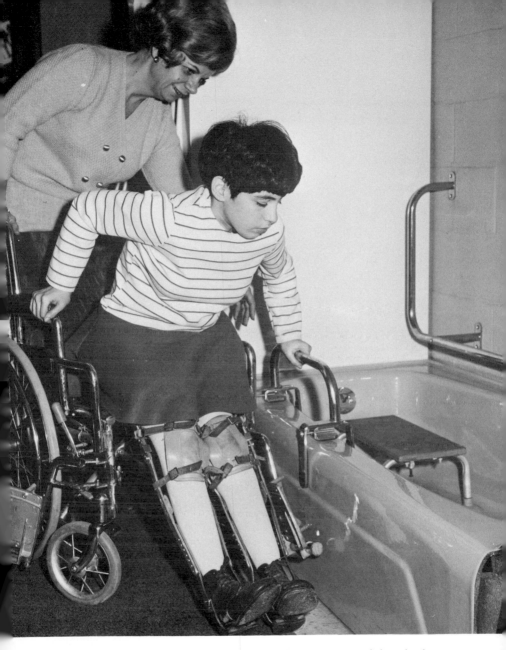

Concepts for personal hygiene and health are an important part of the school curriculum

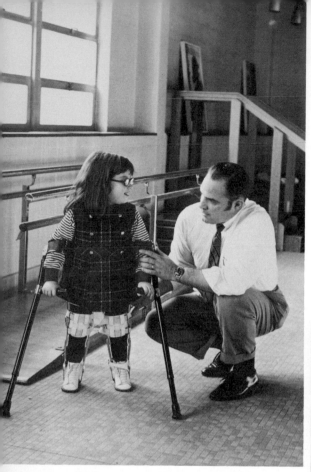

Regular medical care is an essential p
the disabled child's program at Huma
sources School. Longitudinal studies c
child help to determine his abilities an
ticular needs.

Physical therapy sessions encourage the disabled child to maintain a good physical condition and get about on his own.

The specially adapted swimming pool is an important part of the adapted physical education program at Human Resources School. All of the students regardless of their disability can enjoy the freedom afforded by the warm water in games specially designed for them.

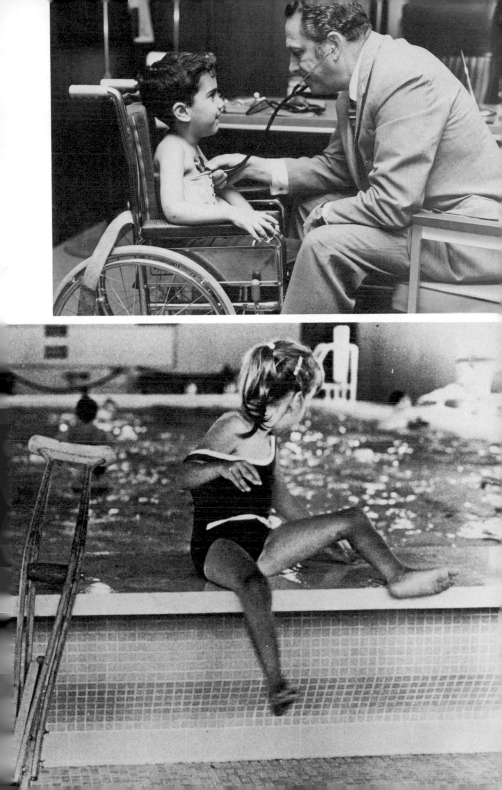

Graduation is a big day at any school but especially at Human Resources School, for it represents years of struggle and determination on the part of the disabled student. Sixty to seventy per cent of each year's graduates go on to college or university of their choice

12

ONE MAN, ONE VOTE

Children, no matter who or what they are have no time for economic or social crises at Christmastime.

Each year at Christmas the younger students of Human Resources School put on a delightful musical play. Working with their teachers, the children stage much of the production themselves. Since many faiths are represented in our school, they pick a neutral theme acceptable to all faiths.

The traditional Nativity play, with the Wise Men and all the rest of that magical Christmas retelling, is treated not as entertainment but as part of religious education. I recall asking one of our students, "Where are you putting on your Nativity play?" And he said, "In our religious class." I asked him what role he played to which he answered with undisguised pride, "I'm one of the wise guys."

The actual musical play is staged for parents and friends, and is performed not only at the Christmas season but also for a second performance at the spring meeting of the Human Resources Board of Governors and their wives. This is a fantastic performance, full of the exuberance of most youthful amateur theatricals. Everyone joins in singing the songs.

The particular production of which I write, and which came to have special meaning to me and to my own future, was called "Annie Get Your Harp." It was written by Joyce Liebman of our music department, and her husband, Art, both highly talented and both of whom have worked in pageants, theatricals and summer camp productions. This was all strictly amateur. The music was mostly borrowed from other sources—pirated would be too strong a word. It was a patchwork of songs all of America at some time has sung. But some of the new children were learning to sing them—on stage!—for the first time in their lives.

One twelve-year-old boy, with crutches firmly in place under both arms, played the part of the Mikado. And a beautiful disabled girl, the Ethel Merman of our school, played Annie, and there were Bat Masterson and other familiar figures that they knew about from television. All these various characters were theirs to act and to be; disabilities notwithstanding, they lived the part as an actor or actress lives the part—of cowboys and outlaws, sheriffs and lovely ladies.

Like all childhood plays, there really has to be a part for everyone. They're either policemen or firemen or jurymen or judges or whatever can be dreamed up. To me, to see them lose themselves in this production, to hear them singing, is something very moving and important. It is wholly personal as an experience, a relationship to these children who are so wonderful, who overcome so much more than we understand.

I realized also, as I watched and listened to that Christmas play in dress rehearsal, that this came at a time when I was caught in our severe struggle to save Abilities, in the pinch of economics, in the struggle for the new school building.

In the darkness of the large assembly room where the final rehearsal was being held, I was torn by the directness of the confrontation. The children cavorting on the stage before me, words and laughter and music and voices filling the auditorium. They were the whole reason; they were tomorrow, they were the future of the work and the cause behind the years. Against that, uppermost among the questions I had to deal with, was the challenge of that overhanging potential nomination for Congress.

I sat watching that dress rehearsal, the voices ringing in my ears. Thoughts tumbled over in my mind. I was concerned about all these pressures with which I lived. To begin a new career could lead on to ever greater things. Or would it lead anywhere at all?

But in those moments in that hall, I was also aware of my own weaknesses, my own failings, things that I, like thousands of other disabled children, lacked in childhood and in many ways still lack. I thought of all the advantages one loses unless they are available in the growing years. I thought of the plays and musicals I and ten thousand like me *didn't* appear in, the songs we didn't sing together as these children were doing here from the school auditorium stage.

I felt at that moment the full awareness of how wrong I would be to run for office when I had these children, this work, this Center, this responsibility as my own special, immediate and all-consuming charge. There were times to change, people to love and help.

The issues and conflicts took on a new focus; outlines seemed sharper, the meanings, the implications. Suppose I should run—and win? Would there not be a conflict of interest? Would I not be representing in Congress, among others, all those who oppose the school, the Center, all those against our plans for the future? Would they not have every right as my constituents to tell Congressman Viscardi exactly what they think of the plans and ideas of Dr. Viscardi who operates the Human Resources Center?

The real goal of life is not personal happiness only, or money, or power over people. The goal must be knowing that you are using your talents to their fullest in some dedicated purpose and direction. If the things we have built over the last two decades or more would be hurt by my walking out for something new, important or not, how could I justify such an act to myself or anyone else?

I would be fifty-nine my next birthday. How many men don't quit when they should? Are there others sufficiently seasoned and experienced now to take over, to carry on? I had, of course, developed other people in the key leadership roles; I have talked about these people. I felt I could rely on them. And the idea of a second career as a national public figure did seem exciting.

But what man can turn his back suddenly on what he is, on his inheritance, on the things one has suffered and stood up against, on causes in which one believes?

If I am changing any life in the field that I know, the field of disability, severe disability, it is because I know the suffering of that life. If I'm changing the course of education so that it can include badly handicapped children it is because I needed something better than homebound courses when I was a child. If I'm trying to break down the barriers of prejudice and ignorance it is because I felt the whiplash of prejudice in my own early life and I'd like to spare some other human being that experience.

Sitting there in the auditorium, I remembered many things. Some of it could be summed up in the word creativity. I had been creative in one sense at least, in the fact that from the shambles of my early years, the hospitals that were my life, my world, I had been able to create something, to shape the individuals and groups who raised the funds and brought into reality this school.

And these children who were, at that very moment, singing, laughing, acting out their roles, were also creating. I am always amazed, for example, in the Art Department, to examine their drawings and water-color paintings, the purple trees and green cows they draw, the enchanting orange-tinted teachers.

Some of the younger children had drawn their impression of me as a child. There was devastating frankness in those pictures. These were very young children, six or seven years old. Little Glenn with total absence of inhibition drew himself and me both in wheelchairs. Another has me standing, apparently talking. And another drew me with an orange nose.

How could I reconcile Washington with these incredible children singing their hearts out, with all their enthusiasm that you could feel even across the rows of seats? What challenge as real as these severely crippled children would be available in Congress? Where would my own life be heading? For what purpose? For children? The world at large? Or for myself?

Then there was the dread of the pending loneliness of being away from Lucile who had been by my side through all these years and in every struggle. The issue itself began to come clearer to me. It was a decision that I had known, from the beginning, was inescapable. As the curtain on the dress rehearsal closed and opened on the children in costume, many of them in their wheel chairs or on crutches, I tried to measure, in my own mind and heart, the depth of my commitment.

Lucile and I talked it over that night. Whatever I decided, she had insisted from the beginning, the decision was mine alone, and whatever it was she would be with me. One thing she did say, however, a number of times, "I want you to do what's right. But I don't want you killing yourself. For this or anything else."

And so we talked it over, Lucile and I—in the light of all these things, these conflicts. In the light of realities that had tumbled over in my mind that day. Abilities was a trouble spot, as Lucile and I both knew, for she had lived through so much of its beginnings, its expansion and now, in the midst of recession and financial difficulties.

And the school which stood behind this concept, the school of children who were to be another demonstration that even the most severely handicapped, the hidden-away children, could be in school, could have normal patterns of activity and could learn to live useful, happy lives, some to marry, to have and rear their own children. Some to die but in their short span of allotted life to have known life in a schoolhouse, in a classroom, with other children. This was the fulfillment of their destiny.

It is not easy to understand these children. Nor is it easy to learn to work with them and their problems. We had one young lady who worked in the school for a six-week period, as part of her college work in education.

She was very disturbed at what she saw in the first days. Her reports of her own experiences began with a note of despair and pessimism. Part of this was due to her own inability to relate directly to the classroom and children. At one early stage she wrote of her own reactions: "One boy in this second class has a terrible skin condition. . . . I must admit that I thought I would get sick. . . . I had terrible guilt feelings afterwards. I don't know what I would do if I were his teacher."

In the weeks that followed, however, her whole attitude changed. There was much that she still didn't understand or found hard to accept. But now she understood that the most basic changes had to come not in the classrooms or the children but within herself. "The end of this week, the end of this month, is both sad and happy for me," she wrote in her final report.

"It is sad because I hate to leave. But it is happy because I've been deeply involved in something which I know I will continue. It could be the beginning of a career."

When we had begun thinking about a school some years earlier, we had little to start on. We had two dozen youngsters for a summer camp program and except for our swimming pool, built as part of the recreation therapy and research programs, we had virtually no facilities. The pool was a major item, of course. But we had no schoolhouse. The children played on the lawn—we had no formal playground facilities.

Out of that we had started the school, and eventually we raised a million dollars with which to build a specially and beautifully designed schoolhouse.

There were limitations; funds only stretched so far. We had one all-purpose room that served as auditorium, gym, luncheon room, meeting hall, recreation room and the setting for commencement exercises. We couldn't hold commencement outside because at certain times we are in the holding pattern for Kennedy Airport and one of the monsters flies over every minute and having commencement outside on the grounds on such nights would have been impossible.

We needed the proposed new building; in my opinion it was absolutely necessary to fulfill the program of education which the school had developed so brilliantly since its opening days. Believing that, we had gone out and raised money from many sources and individuals who believed in our goals. There are many who support our cause, but the task of fund raising is still a task. We set the goal of the building itself, including a gymnasium, cafeteria area, a stage and other physical facilities, at $1,800,000. I estimated in addition that we needed another $1,200,000 to start our endowment fund. Later, as inflationary pressures continued, I lifted the total figure to three and a half million dollars.

As this is written, we have raised in cash and securities within $300,000 of our goal.

The funds were there, out of blood and sweat and meetings and all that goes with the arduous job of raising money. The new building and its important facilities could be built. If, that is, they would let us do it, if the neighbors would allow this plan to come to reality for these children and their future.

But the other question was still there, to be met, to be finally answered: Did I really want to run for that job in Congress, the broader challenge of the national field. The answer was yes, I did. But could I accept it? The answer was no. I couldn't accept because I couldn't turn my back on these people, on this center, on these children in whom I saw a reflection of myself as a crippled child. I couldn't live with myself if I turned my back on them or on people like Alex and all the other adults I had worked with all these years.

The political arena, the national scene, the excitement of all that was of compelling force. Yet a force even stronger in my mind resided in the challenge of changing for the better the lives of children like these, of giving hope to them and their families, of changing the ground rules and expectations for tens of thousands of such children all over this nation and the world. And this I realized was a richer destiny than being a congressman or Secretary of State, Vice-President or even President.

Thus the battle was about to be joined, in the hearing that lay ahead before the Town Board—the neighbors and their attorneys on one side, the children and those voices, their words, songs and laughter on the other.

And so we talked it over, Lucile and I. And I wrote a letter.

I wrote this letter actually on December 23rd, two days before Christmas. It was addressed to my good friend and sponsor, the Hon. John D. Caemmerer. This letter declared:

"I am hopeful that you will understand my delay in responding to the suggestion that I become available as a candidate for the House of Representatives. It has not been a simple, easily reached decision, especially in view of the responsibilities I face as founder and chief executive of Human Resources Center and serving the cause of crippled people to whom I have devoted my life.

"In seeking advice from friends and associates close to me and from my family, I have decided not to seek this high office. You understand how regretfully this decision is reached after the most prayerful consideration.

"The work of Human Resources Center has now

reached the peak in the preparation for construction of the central building of our campus which, hopefully, will be started this spring. Human Resources School, the Research and Training Institute and Abilities workshop each have vigorous, young leaders, who are now being groomed as successors. . . . It is too soon for me to leave them. . . . The time in our growth is too critical.

"Thank you for suggesting that I consider this possibility to serve our country. I have such great faith in the cause for America in these unusual times. This incessant attention to our problems and weaknesses should be changed to encouragement and hope that we can overcome our difficulties. If we lose faith in ourselves we will only become what our critics say we are.

"Please extend to your colleagues my deep gratitude for their belief in me and in the dreams which I have nourished and protected through bad days where, for so many disabled Americans, they are now coming true. . . ."

This letter was delivered to the Senator by messenger. The pressures continued to increase, however, in behalf of my changing my mind. At last, I wrote another letter reaffirming my original stand and my original reasons for taking this action.

Another Christmas moment helped to shape that decision—Christmas Eve, 1969, when, NBC televised a color sequence at Human Resources Center, a brief segment of what and who we are, winding up with me sitting in shirtsleeves behind my desk in my office, reflecting for the TV cameras on love and human dignity.

I was told that this was a very moving telecast. Certainly it reached a wide audience of millions of adults and children on that Christmas Eve. And some of those viewers wrote to us at Abilities. One letter came to me from the mother of one of our children in the school, a very simple warm letter, telling how much she appreciated what I had done, what all of us in the Center have done, for children like hers, and how much this means to her and her husband—and her severely disabled daughter. How wonderful it has been for the child, she said, that we had been able to give her a whole new horizon, a whole new meaning to her life.

The echoes of my anticipated public activity and law-making die in the distance. Perhaps one day the situation will change; there could be a time for such things, for this wider range of action at the heart of the national scene.

In the meantime we at Human Resources Center faced the challenges of here and now, in the raucous hearing we were to face—the educational-cultural zoning hearing, on the outcome of which so much of the future role of the school and its children depended.

13

PLANS AND PERSPECTIVES

ılıılılılılılılılılılılılılılılılılılılılılılılılılılılılılılılılılılılılılılılılılılılılılılılılılılılılılılılılılılılılılılıl

At this crucial time my life and work seemed almost like a series of battles waged simultaneously, each with its own urgency and direction. They had to be put into a proper perspective. The hearing, in preparation for which the Albertson protest group were busy sending out teams to build opposition to our plans for the school and the children, loomed as the most important. And unquestionably the most emotional.

Sometimes answers and new perspectives come in unexpected ways and unlooked-for words. Only a few days after I had made my final, irrevocable decision on the issue of my running for Congress, in the very midst of all these difficulties at Human Resources, I happened to be reading a transcript of words uttered by a twelve-year-old boy as tape-recorded by a therapist working with blind children. In order to achieve full spontaneity, the boy, blind from birth, was not told until afterwards that the words were being recorded. Yet some of his words did throw a new perspective—a blind boy's perspective—on the underlying realities of some immediate problems:

"There are many things in this world," the blind boy declared, "that people could reach out and touch and keep a part of them, for their very own, and spread it around for everyone. Not money because money is only good for what it can do, only good if it is used to help. But people could reach out for kindness and fair play, and could spread it around for others.

"I've heard on the radio all this talk about integration in the schools, to give all children a chance to go to school together. And there seems to be such a fuss about it because some of the children are different, and I can't understand at all what this difference is.

"They say it is their color and what is color? I guess I'm lucky that I cannot see differences in color because it seems to me that the kind of hate that these people put in their minds must chase out all chance to grow in understanding. . . ."

This boy was in effect talking about not many stories but one. Unable himself to distinguish light from dark or black from white, he was talking about all peoples, all colors, all races, conditions. And each situation, whether relating to school or business, to child or adult, to black or white, able or disabled, blind or sighted, was important. The time had come to reexamine where we were—to press forward with the work of this Center.

Abilities was a number one problem. There was a little progress, however, to promote new business, particularly in the field of our banking operations. Art was handling these plans in consultation with me. We knew that the operation had to turn around to show profits instead of losses. The specific need was to develop new business, new workloads, providing major industry with expert work at prices they could also afford. Contracts in the electronic field had been slow to come in.

Much of the future of Abilities, as Art and I saw it, lay in the abiding promise of the computers. Here, our people could serve excellently, not only our disabled workers but also the group of retarded employees. We had begun the employment of retarded more than ten years earlier, in some of our banking operations begun in association with the Franklin National Bank.

We had plans for a banking and computerized world at Abilities. We had been convinced for many years that data preparation for computers was the future, both for ourselves and for others. If the children in Human Resources School were to compete in a real world they had to relate to a world of data processing and computer sciences.

With the development of remote terminals and scanning devices feeding directly into a computer, new opportunities for the disabled were presented. Our age levels at the Center range from three-year olds to eighty-five and the range of disabilities covers the whole field of classifications, including catastrophic disabilities, multiple handicaps, geriatrics, the blind, even the retarded, who were included in the Abilities workshop where they had been trained successfully as key-punch operators, bank clerks and electronic assemblers.

All this was part of our story: Buildings, classrooms, gyms, food for our children, food for adults, recreation, health, safety, research, and work benches and machines. And the future lay in the dreams that still live within all of us—all of our people.

Those who oppose us seem almost to fear our success. They fear that somehow, by what we are doing for our people, we are draining the community. They do not consider that we bring much *to* the community in new wealth and increased property values.

They look at us and say: "Why aren't you paying taxes to help us with our tax burdens?" Of course, what they don't look at is 1967, 1966, 1965 when we didn't earn nearly as much as we had previously; or 1970 when instead of an excess our loss figures and investments in new ventures ran over a half million dollars. Nor is there any consideration of the tremendous investments in rehabilitation, training, new buildings, and equipment, none of which cost the local community any money. Nor of the economic return to the community of the disabled who become taxpayers instead of having to be supported.

So their fears build and add up, their fears about us and about their taxes and a dozen other factors.

Can we actually change the situation? Could we plan new avenues to victory? No one can answer this, speaking specifically of prejudice in the world we have to live with and deal with. I think we have made some dents in the general situation, in the usual and familiar attitudes encountered, the subterfuges, the subtle circumlocutions.

We have made a start but I think our problem will take much longer to change than will that of the blacks. The black people have fought for and already have won new and strong footholds in the area of equality of opportunity. It is a long way indeed from real equality, either in this country or elsewhere, but strides have been made by their programs, their action, the publicity, their group cohesion and organization.

In regard to the disabled, however, we find on one hand compassion for the handicapped and a willingness to do something to support us, but too little or no willingness to give us equality of opportunity to support ourselves, little or no desire really to change attitudes. I suppose it is not because people do not care but because they are involved with other pressures and problems in industry, in schools, in the community. There are so many problems that this one can apparently be ignored.

Perspectives have become diffuse and uncertain. Few builders are willing to pay hard cash to overcome the headache of designing an apartment house or railroad station or an airplane or a community on a wholly new basis, with adequate elevators and doors wide enough for wheel chairs, for example, so that disabled people can come in and go out like other people. Architects design buildings for majorities, not minorities.

Yet I remember the paraplegic colonel in Korea

who wouldn't dream of spending his life in a wheel chair but had a bearer whose sole duty was to carry the colonel on his shoulders wherever the colonel went, and who would set him down in a chair and cut his food for him and feed him. While there are increasing examples of progress, for many disabled millions life is unrewarding and hopeless.

In the days after my decision, I searched for directions and for perspectives to guide me. Some of these were clear and definite; others were blurred, unsure, distorted.

What we were seeing in the immediate community concerned attitudes and beliefs. It was a pattern shaped of desperate uncertainties, of taxes continuing to soar until they could no longer be borne, of rising commuter rates, of the rising tide of black people moving into the white communities because the blacks also could no longer accept ghettos. And the whites striking out blindly in their terror. "They will bring their ghettos and their fury with them. . . ."

So much is built up, stirred up, mounted into major issues. It becomes a frightening human game of move and countermove. Black parents move to have their children bused to an integrated school where they can actually experience the sense of brotherhood, of community, sitting together, side by side in a classroom. And the white parents, with what they consider perfectly valid reasons, boycott the buses and demand to know why their children must be bused to remote schools while schools are available in their own communities. Busing is put forward as one partial solution to racial problems; in some areas it has worked well. But there are other areas where it has intensified rather than ameliorated tensions and confrontations.

When I think of the problem of the blacks, I cry out for the disabled black, for he is forgotten even by his own people who can do little or nothing for him. Of all the people in the underprivileged area he is the last to be considered, the least likely to be given an opportunity to be educated, to be trained and to find work.

I weep for the black crippled children in our school as I do for all crippled children, for I seek a world in which they will be accepted and I know they have the added burden in life.

The big payoff, the real challenge is not in school but in life. The disabled adult who has been trained in Abilities must find a job one day on the outside, in the real world. And if he is black and disabled, he faces two quotas, two prejudices which he must overcome.

Nothing is ever said outright, not in this area. The words take on non-abrasive disguises—economic, practical, legal, educational. "We don't want to hear the noise of screeching tires" becomes a transliteration for an underlying emotional reaction that many throughout a community, throughout the world, really feel: "The cries and laughter of crippled children at play is a saddening, disturbing sound."

It is fear, of course. Fear that it could happen to them. Fear of contagion. Would you want your sister to marry a paraplegic? A Jew? A Mexican? Do we have to see them in our neighborhood?

I understood. Deeply and wholly and completely I understood.

I understood also, from all reports coming in, the mounting anger of the neighbors around us. Whipped up by a handful of leaders and by an attorney who came on loud and clear, blustering, assailing, demanding, they were ready to carry on their fight as far as they had to go. They were not about to retreat an inch. They were out in the community building their support with the residents, door to door. To be for Abilities and Human Resources Center was to be in favor of the enemy.

The main hearing we were to have in the North Hempstead Town Hall was only days ahead. We had prepared carefully for this; our attorneys had drawn up full reports on what we were striving for, what our plans were, how the area would be landscaped. We had drawings of the underground garage we planned, and could show how, far from creating traffic problems, it would achieve a reduction of traffic and parking problems in the whole area. The educational-cultural zoning would allow for a five-story tower if we wanted it in the future and would be in the center of the area, set well back from the boundary of our property. It would not block the view or light of any resident or home. Five stories were not, however, included in our immediate building plans, which called for only two stories, well within the present allowable rights.

We had, in fact, done all that we could to make this plan a contribution to the community, a beautiful, interesting, useful setting that my associates and I believed would enhance any neighborhood.

Some of the neighbors did not agree. They were angry, they were militant.

Newspapers around us carried a number of stories of the meetings and plans to stir up action against us. The gatherings were held in various homes, or in open meetings in local halls. The leaders were out beating the bushes, making sure a large group would be on hand. It was the pattern that had been developed as a technique in committees throughout the frustrated, frightened world of suburbia, a pattern of stormy, over-crowded meetings, of people protecting themselves against the encroaching needs of other peoples, children and aged, black and brown, retarded, disabled.

The struggle was both financial and political. Faced in all its said and unsaid implications, we had proven that severely handicapped men and women didn't have to beg or whine or live second-class citizens' lives; we had proven over nearly two decades that they could earn a living, could do a day's work for a day's pay, comply with production standards and levels of the toughest competition and the most sophisticated technology in industry. We had proven the whole thing. We had made it work.

But now we were learning something else. That even with all of this we remained the unwanted. Even with all our achievements, all of these years of work and proof of what we were, and what we could do, they wanted us out.

The hearing at North Hempstead Town Hall was only days ahead. Newspapers reported that hundreds of residents would be there to protest our plans. The whole meaning of lives, of our right to exist at all, appeared at that moment precariously at stake.

14

ENEMY OF THE PEOPLE

Throngs of protesters stormed the Town Hall of North Hempstead, Long Island, that chill morning in the winter of 1970. They came noisily and angrily; it was more of a mob scene than a normal Town Board meeting. They came literally by the hundreds, their anger and fears fanned by the meetings, petitioners, and door-to-door canvassing teams. If you weren't against Mr. Viscardi's ambitious new plans, how could you be a good citizen of this community?

We had several of our staff people there plus our own attorney, John F. Coffey, and one or two of the graduates from our school. None of our school children attended. The neighbors outnumbered us by fifty to one or better. They crowded in around us; there was a sense of purpose about this throng. This was their day to spell it all out, to put it all together.

We had not solicited an attendance. Anyone who wanted to come was welcome. There were only our staff people and some of the old-time people from Abilities, like Alex, Frank Gentile and Jim Gellat.

We were not only the enemy in a very real sense, we

were the symbol of all the enemies. We wanted to build skyscrapers, they said. Towers into the Albertson skies. Our beautifully designed school and campus plans would ruin the whole community, wreck property values and destroy peace and calm and safety.

Some of our younger student-teachers who were either volunteers or holdovers from summer faculty attended the night session of this frontal attack on our programs and future. (The number of witnesses who wanted to be heard made the night session essential; this also gave the head of the family time to get home for dinner before coming around to add his voice to the others.) What these young volunteers witnessed was a mob scene. One of them told me afterwards he had seen only one other mob scene in his life—a night at Roosevelt Raceway when he watched from the upper stands as people below lunged out wildly. He had the same feeling at this hearing.

Of course, the people crowding into Town Hall committed no illegal or violent acts. But an underlying mob spirit was there. They had been whipped up in their anger. Among the college students who attended the hearing was Rick McCarthy who directed our summer camp programs. He and all of our faculty were accustomed to our atmosphere of love for our children. "I watched two individuals. They had Florida tans and they wore flaming shirts and both were positioned strategically in that hearing room," Rick reported. "They had grating voices and words of denunciation, all the time insisting that they loved us, loved our children. But on cue, if our attorney, our medical adviser, our architect, even the mothers of the children in our school, tried to explain, on cue these voices came.

"They used language you would never permit in your own home, let alone in a public hearing-place. They were there to destroy any understanding. That was the point, you see. They did not want understanding. Over and over the same phrases and words, sometimes almost as if they were a litany: "We don't want to hurt the children. We love the children. We're for the good work at the Center, but we don't want this building. We don't want this tower."

Throughout the entire day, the people crowding into the aisles, lining the walls, lining the back of the room, kept up the constant din of interruptions, questions, wisecracks, interpretations, noisy side comments.

At one point while I was making my own statement to the Board on the background of the situation and why we needed our school building, there was such an outbreak of disruptive cries and denunciations, that Chairman Meade had to halt the proceedings to get order. "What is the point back there?" he demanded.

The voices were noisy and raucous, many people were talking at once. Many kept insisting that they weren't really against us at all. "We welcome them . . . We love their work. . . . We are not quarreling about that."

"We live with Abilities, and we respect Abilities, and we love their work. We have no objection."

"He doesn't have to justify Abilities to us. We live

with them, we love them. We recognize this."

"We don't actually want a six-story building. That's why we are here."

"That's right."

Loud applause again interrupted the proceedings. All of this was going on, let me note, while I was officially recognized and in the process of formally explaining to the Town Board why we were in favor of the educational-cultural zoning, and why we wanted authorization for the addition to our school.

Supervisor Meade, disturbed by the disorder, demanded that each speaker be given courtesy.

Somebody cried out at that, "For how long?"

"I think that might be a test of courtesy," the Supervisor said. Then he added quietly, "I also might mention, while I have this opportunity, in view of the crowd, that I would appreciate no smoking in the room. Would you proceed, Mr. Viscardi?"

Proceed I did, despite the continued harassment of the mob. Certainly I had a right to say the things I had to say. I had a right to be heard in orderly fashion, to state our case, why we existed and what we did, and what we stood for. This is a right supposedly of any citizen in any public hearing, under the rules of law and order. Are not these the rights we in America believe in?

"Let me take a moment to talk about the school," I began at one point, when a voice broke in loudly, "Mr. Meade. . . ." I tried to go on. "In the Human Resources School, we have a population of. . . ."

"A point of order, sir." And then, "I would like to

apologize for my rudeness, really. . . ." The interruptions continued.

I had to stop speaking. The voice went on to set up the idea that since they knew all this old-hat stuff anyway, what business or right did I have to try to present the Board our case for existing, for growing, for expanding?

"Since I think the majority of the people present are really very gracious to Abilities, and we recognize the facts, possibly this report could be submitted in writing for the Board, since we know most of it, and we do accept it."

"We recognize their good work," someone else broke in.

There was further applause.

The Supervisor stated finally: "I might also repeat my request about no smoking."

"We don't want a six-story building," a woman cried out. "That's why we're here."

Referring to me, provoked to anger, the Supervisor said calmly, "Once more, Mr. Viscardi, will you proceed, please."

Someone shouted about a point of order, but there was no point of order, actually. Nor was there order at all. There was only a continuing effort to stop me from stating our case to the Board.

Once again, I tried to proceed. "In connection with Human Resources School, we have a student population of approximately 176 children. These represent major disabilities, which have precluded these children from going to school. Our Human Resources

School is accepted as a pilot demonstration project, under a special act of the State of New York.   .

"The School begins with the pre-school program of three- and four-year-olds, and goes right on through high school. I would call to your attention that these are children who would not have gone to school, but would have been homebound. I would like to indicate, for the record, that if these students were still on homebound instruction in their school districts, it would have cost these districts $680,000 last year and $2,276,000 since the school began in 1962."

I went on trying to finish my argument for approval for our petition, why we needed the new building, the new zoning. I did manage to finish, despite the din of continuous interruptions and heckling. I was disgusted at the exhibition staged during our attempt to present our case. Believing in this as I did, I could not subject myself to further abuse at the hands of these people.

As I left the crowded hearing room, with Jim Gellat running interference for me through the throng, members of the angry mob still continued their verbal assault: "Keep him here!". . . ."Don't let him get away!". . . ."Why is he leaving?"

They needed a victim. And the victim despite them was walking out on his sturdy artificial limbs.

We love you;—we really love Abilities. That was the phrase. It was an old litany, an empty litany we have heard many times in our lives.

A number of other witnesses spoke for us, despite all the interruptions and asides coming from the mob crowding in.

The opposition's case was one of bringing in the experts and neighbors to denounce one phase or another of our plans. Behind the outcries of their arguments, behind the words of many speakers, was a secondary theme, made specifically to Board members—that they had better be deeply concerned because the protesters were voters and the voters wouldn't go along with any Board member who voted in favor of Abilities. It was a power play: Don't vote in conscience what you believe to be right or wrong. Vote our way—or else.

At one point the choices were made quite explicit. In presenting his clients' case, which was based primarily on changing the zoning to make it an "educational and cultural" area, the attorney for the opposition commented that he had heard there was a possibility that Supervisor Meade might be picked for a State Supreme Court judgeship. If this were so, he said, he wished the supervisor all the best, and urged that he leave behind his administration something to be proud of which he indicated did not include—in his own description—"a five-story building in a residential area." (The truth was that we had no application for building five stories—only two.)

The attorney very skillfully laid the groundwork. A few minutes later, in closing his argument, he urged the Board members to oppose our application, specifically citing those Board members who, he noted pointedly, "will have to run again" and who "may not be appointed to the Supreme Court so soon."

Should there be any doubt as to what he meant, the attorney reiterated his warning: "Those of you who

have to run again, remember, we are the people. We
ask you to oppose this application."

Don't vote the right thing as you see it. Vote as we
tell you to vote.

At one point in the extraordinary, if not bizarre,
proceedings, our attorney, Mr. Coffey, put our architect for the new building, Sigmund Spiegel, on the
stand. He was the designer of the original Human
Resources School, which has been called one of the
finest examples of special educational facilities in the
world. He described himself as being licensed to prac-
tice in eleven states as well as being a licensed professional planner in the state of New Jersey.

"I designed, several years ago," he stated, "the cur-
rent Human Resources School, and this has given
me a great deal of insight in how to design for the
disabled. We are at this point contemplating a
building. . . ."

"Mr. Spiegel, where do you live?" Someone broke
in.

"North Bellmore," the architect responded to the
voice.

"Just a point," the voice said.

"Would you continue, Mr. Spiegel, please" The
supervisor said, "Again I would ask that everybody
extend as much courtesy as possible."

"Spare us the commercials," came another anony-
mous voice.

Again and again, while the architect was trying to
present the rationale of his design, and to show how
it would be anything but ugly, anything but indus-

trial, he was interrupted by persons who insisted upon being answered then and there. Frequently, in an effort to keep the proceedings moving, our attorney Mr. Coffey did supply information asked for, even though it was not the time for such questions, even though it was in the midst of the architect's presentation of his design and its purposes. .

Bitterness and anger deepened as the proceedings continued. There were long periods when there was no chance at all for the people to be heard. This was particularly true in the evening session, after the commuting husbands had arrived home and discussed it with their wives over the cocktail hour and a hurried dinner. Much of the testimony was not only interrupted by intermittent barrages of questions from speakers who did not wait to be recognized, but in addition the continuing din of side comments and other discourtesies made it impossible for the overflow crowd in the outer halls to hear anything.

The tumult and shouting did not die, but some of the voices did get heard finally. One witness who supported our petition—she was the mother of a handicapped child, in fact, and had also adopted another handicapped child—pointed out some of the facts of life regarding parents like herself and her husband, and children like theirs.

"We have dreams too for our children and their future, just as you do," she told the gathering. "But there are many children," she added, "who attend Human Resources School who cannot go to other schools, who . . . cannot hope to compete.

"These children have to be trained in a special way. The facilities of Abilities are made available to these children.

"They are taught computer programming, data processing, and all jobs which are very, very important to the handicapped, because a handicapped person is very suited to this type of work. . . ."

Her calmness did make itself felt in the room; there was a noticeable lack of interruptions while she spoke. It was not that they agreed with her. But perhaps the spirit of motherhood had its effect, in spite of the deep-rooted disagreement. The mother, in any case, did not pull her punches.

I think I can guess what was in that woman's heart as she spoke to this gathering. She was speaking impromptu. She was not a professional speaker, and had not often talked to such a gathering as this, I am very sure. And yet she was able to express herself and her meaning as articulately as any who spoke that day. She recognized also the economic issue involved in the protests, the fear that had been spread that somehow our buildings would decrease land values—a concept disproved completely by the history of increased values in the community since our center started. In her closing sentences she spoke of that underlying economic concern:

"I may be over thirty," she told them, "but I certainly understand the young people, and the young people know that when you hit the parents in the pocketbook, that's when they squawk. They can sit in their living room and say, 'Look at those poor children

in Biafra.' And they can say, 'Look at this terrible
thing.'

"You people aren't against handicapped children,
but you're certainly not for them, either."

There was applause again—from some of those who
supported us.

I think that many of these people were simply mis-
taken and misled. The controversy may have played
upon certain forces within themselves. I think that
you can play up fear, that you can build patterns of
fear, and patterns that grow out of fear. One woman
objector at the hearings seemed suddenly to have
found a whole new fear—that of being made to look
like the "bad guys" because of their attack on us and
our school and our plans. She simply could not understand why we saw them in such a light.

Paul Hearne who was graduated from our school,
was President of both the Senior Class and the Student Council and he later became President of the
Human Resources School Alumni Association. He is
also president of the Student Government at Hofstra
University.

I asked Paul if he would care to take time from his
college classes to appear at the hearing in North
Hempstead Town Hall and tell his side of the case of
the new school building and, as reflected in the school
itself, the whole Human Resources purpose. Paul said
nothing could keep him away. And he was there that
day addressing the Board from his mobile litter. Even
the angry people understood that here they would
have to hold their peace, their sarcasm, while this col-

lege student on a litter made his statement.

And indeed, it was something for them to listen to, for Paul is more articulate than most young people.

"Our parents were new in this experience, too," he declared at one point, "We, who left the house formerly only on rare occasions, were now going to school every day.

"We were learning for ourselves how to interpret the world, instead of asking our parents. Our self-sufficiency and independence were the ideas now predominant in our parents' minds, not despair.

"The world outside was no longer an image; it was a reality. . . .

"In my senior year, in Human Resources School, I constructed an amateur radio station. Being the holder of an amateur radio license, I began the task of teaching amateur radio courses, preparing students for a Federal Operator's License. Since then six students have passed the examinations qualifying them for licenses. A station is now on the air, in contact with other operators all over the world. The vistas of these students are further widened beyond the school to their contacts, on a varied and international basis. Now, Russia, Japan, and even China can learn of our unique school, and they do so with an interest that eliminates political barriers."

One of the moments he related to the Board and the throng of neighbors at the meeting was the fact that the station actually made amateur radio contact with another "ham" operator thousands of miles distant— Barry Goldwater. The Senator and former presiden-

tial candidate, speaking with the amateur radio frater-
nity answered simply to the name "Barry."

Perhaps most important in Paul Hearne's remarks were a few paragraphs on his own personal
views. These were not merely the words of a college youth trying to find something significant to
say. They had a depth that runs beyond the average
student, beyond the seeming simplicity of his
words:

"In an age of dissent, war, hunger, and man's
general inhumanity to man, it is an encouraging
fact to see people help people to help themselves.
The words 'freedom' and 'opportunity' mean much
more when they are not attached to any individual
point of view, because only if someone senses their
values for someone besides themselves can they
bear their true meaning.

"It is frightening to me to wonder where my
graduating class would be today, if it were not for
Human Resources School. A school is only a con-
glomerate of brick and cement, without those people within it, this school *is* the people within it.
Human Resources School has created a good which
cannot be slowed or stopped, only furthered. This
good must be furthered. It is no longer a question
of problems affecting anyone in the present. It can
now be a question of morality.

"Therefore, I hereby urge you to vote a loud
'yes' to approve this building and be a part of
tomorrow's future."

There was a scattering of applause. Supervisor

Meade informed the young man on the litter, "I am sure that everyone in this room applauds you for your accomplishments today."

The protesting neighbors returned once more to the tactics of heckling and parlimentary disorder. It went on this way throughout the afternoon and evening sessions.

At last, in the late hours of the North Hempstead night, the Town Board ended the long bitter day by agreeing to take the Human Resources School rezoning petition under advisement.

15

DECISION IN SUBURBIA

The weeks that followed became a time of waiting, of tension. I did not know most of the members on the Town Board; I could only hope that they were sound, responsible citizens who would not be intimidated by suggestions that a wrong decision might cost them votes. The educational-cultural zoning idea had been largely sponsored by town government. And in our opinion their position was a good one. If the Town Board approved the zoning, our application would go through, since we had applied under the proposed zoning change.

But as days and weeks dragged on with no action, no findings, the tightening suspense also grew. It was a strange, quiet period, this waiting, for us at Human Resources and I suppose also for those who opposed us.

In the immediate vicinity of Human Resources, there was no outward sign of tension but it was there underneath; the raucous performance of the immediate neighbors at that meeting still clung in the atmosphere. And despite the meeting, I was sure the majority of our immediate neighbors had not been supporters of the group. One man in particular wished me luck. He had been at the meeting and had left in what he described as "total disgust."

"Maybe they thought they were wholly right about it all," he told me, "but I don't. What's more, the way they acted was a disgrace. That is all you could call it —a disgrace."

Of course, we had the other kind of call too—the call denouncing us and saying we were just trying to "put something over" for our own purposes.

And there were rumors. The rumor mills had it that the Town Board was going to find for us but would indulge in delaying tactics because of the upcoming elections. There were stories that the Board would vote against us unanimously. People peddling that story pointed out that it had been years and years since any local town board in the Long Island area had split its vote. All the votes were unanimous.

There were also rumors that many other groups fighting for special causes, popular or unpopular, were watching this action of ours closely. Our struggle in North Hempstead apparently was an important case because kindred controversies were being fought out in other towns. There were requests to build facilities for the retarded, the aged, the brain-damaged. The intensity with which every issue was fought, whatever it was about, added to the tension with which our own case was being watched.

So we waited. And elsewhere other people waited, in one community or the next, for one town board or another, in one challenge for human dignity or another. Consider one example—the case of a proposed school for emotionally disturbed children, to be built in a remote area in the community of Baldwin, Long Island.

The Nassau County Board of Cooperative Educational Services had informed Baldwin authorities that the school had to have a new location, that the present quarters for the emotionally disturbed children, a converted factory in Hicksville, was outmoded and wholly unsuitable and that the children had to stand waiting in long lines even to go to the toilet.

Baldwin's town supervisor had worked out a plan to let the school be built on an unused sixteen-acre strip taken out of a Baldwin park area of nearly one hundred and fifty acres. Many Baldwin residents at once were in an uproar over the situation, however. The familiar rounds of meetings, lawyers and organized dissent was set in motion. One report suggested that after they got the school in, a narcotics treatment center in the park would probably be the next move.

Long Island news reporters also scurried around talking to other neighbors in the area and came up with another perspective on sources of dissension in Baldwin. ". . . Two persons close to the community, both of whom have requested anonymity rather than face the wrath of constitutents and neighbors," one news story declared, "give different reasons for the opposition."

The news account went on: " 'You'll never get them to admit it, even to themselves,' said a professional

who knows that community, 'but they are hysterical
at the thought of having a school for emotionally disturbed children near them. You cannot talk to them
about it because they will deny it. It just doesn't fit
their self-image as liberal people.

"And a resident who has lived in the community for
more than a decade gave another reason: 'You have to
understand that most of these people are business people, and a lot of their money is in their homes. We're
in a recession now, maybe the beginnings of a depression, and that equity is all that a lot of them have.
They'll fight anything they think might threaten to
reduce it. They're afraid that if the school goes into
the park and brings the traffic with it, their property
values will go down.' The speaker paused. 'Some of
them are just plain afraid of the school, but they won't
admit it.' A longer pause: 'I've lived here a long time,
but if you use my name, they'll run me out of town on
a rail.' "

And so black and white, crippled and whole, retarded and normal, waited for people and boards and
officials to act. And we waited with them, each for his
cause.

Days went on, and there was no word. There were
moments when we felt it was almost deliberate delay,
almost a desire to draw the string as tight as it would
go without snapping. We heard one rumor that this
was a deliberate tactic, that they wanted us on edge,
those who protested, that their plan was to drag it out,
as long as possible, to keep us in such a state that we
would surrender any plans we had to expand.

From their words at the hearing, it was clear that they did have some such approach. It was clear that their intentions went beyond merely halting expansion. Part of the argument was that Human Resources Center was really illegal, that we were a manufacturing business for profit rather than a school, work and training center, pilot project or research center.

In my heart I was certain that it went further; that they really and truly wanted us gone, that we didn't belong. We were the intruders, the whole center, the whole impossible dream.

The time did have to arrive, of course, when the Board would act. It came on a lovely suburban morning in late spring. The decision was received with the greatest anticipation by everyone at Human Resources Center.

The result was precisely the same in our case as in the case of the black group who worked so hard to support their proposed low-cost housing project.

The answer was the same—the vote the same. It was four to one against us—and four to one against the project. It is difficult to imagine a more direct slap across the faces of two groups of handicapped people and black people.

One could almost wonder if there was some reason for the decisions. Perhaps it was to let minorities understand that basically they could not expect rights or needs to be protected, if contra-indicated by other considerations.

In any event, the facts were that the Town Board had turned down wholly the proposed change for an educational and cultural zoning law, and with this we had been turned down utterly in our application to erect a new school building under that change.

There was one speck of daylight in all of that—the single negative vote in each instance, the vote cast by Supervisor Meade. This was an exemplary and immeasurable act of political courage. The fact that Supervisor Meade dared to cast his vote in dissent in both decisions was a startling one throughout the community. It was more than a vote of courage, it was one of defiance, not against the will of the people but against the vote of political expediency in the face of the mob. Some would have called it an act of sheer political madness to vote against all his associates on the Town Board. But Meade had no apologies to make. He stood his ground totally unyielding, totally unafraid.

Was he destroying himself by this action? I believe this: Whether he was destroying his political career or not did not influence his decision of what was right. Some time after the decision of the Board, I met the Supervisor and asked him if he did not feel that his political career in the community might be damaged or finished because he voted for us rather than against us as the others did.

In very deliberate words, the Supervisor answered: "No. It's a matter of principle. I had no choice but to send in the dissenting opinion, and if that destroys me, that's all right, too. I'll make it some other way. But this should be done."

A newspaper story on the decisions described

Supervisor Robert Meade delivering his vote "with the extra firm voice of a nervous bridegroom."

Perhaps they meant a bridegroom of truth.

"Typically, Meade had no harsh words for the other board members," the story went on. "He said that he didn't feel out on a political limb, 'but sometimes I feel kind of lonesome.' Integrity is a word used by political friend and foe when describing Meade, who summed up his commitments to the two issues by quoting John Gardner, head of the national Urban Coalition: 'We must call for the best or live with the worst.' "

In brief encounter and exchange of a handful of sentences with the Supervisor, I grasped the full depth of earnest conviction that he had done what was right, that he was not about to surrender on a point in which he believed.

One feels outrage in such moments. But not hate for one's opponents. I felt none in my heart. The people doing this, if we examine the whole pattern closely, think they have good reasons. They have been led to believe their reasons. Their aversion, their prejudice is largely latent. They would deny it exists. They couldn't admit it openly because they don't recognized it as such.

We were not going to let this thing die. Within a few days after the April decision against us by the Town Board, Jack Coffey took a new step. He made a request for a building permit to the North Hempstead Board of Zoning and Appeals. This board was constituted to accept jurisdiction and to review the application and render their own verdict as a new request.

We could have gone this route at first but elected to ride under the hearings on the proposed educational-cultural zoning changes. Now we had to start anew and new hearings would be held as though the ones just completed never existed. The fight was on again.

Early in July the Nassau County Planning Commission, after examination of our plans and drawings, approved our entire building program. Shortly thereafter, another hearing was held by the Board of Zoning Appeals on the application. Once again the protesters moved in, once again parents of our students spoke on our behalf. Once again our people had to undergo unbelievable heckling, distortions and abuse.

At this later hearing, we decided it was best if our attorney, John Coffey, stayed away from the hearing, simply to remove an obvious target for the opposition, since Coffey, as I, had been built up as a prime symbol of the enemy. One of Coffey's associates took over.

Even so, we kept in close contact throughout the long hearing. In the early evening, three of us—Frank Gentile, Jim Gellat and myself discussed the fact that the opposition all through the late afternoon kept hammering away at the concept that our computer training program was actually going to be a big money-making operation that planned to concentrate not on training but on bringing in outside business.

This was not the fact. We were going to bring in some outside business for two reasons: to help defray the cost of the operation and to help develop on-the-job training for our people, a successful training approach we had used since the first day we opened our shop.

However, we won on this point by a sudden switch which we relayed to our people at the evening hearing for immediate announcement. Since there was some objection raised to our computers going into the new building, we would leave that part of our training program where it was in the center. This was a simple matter. The announcement of this sudden change in our plans to meet one of the objections came at the summation. They had been going great guns on this computer situation until suddenly the issue was no longer there and there was nothing left for them to shoot at in that direction.

It was not, perhaps, the absolute, decisive issue but it helped greatly in the final analysis. And it certainly smothered some of the wind in the opposition sails.

The final act this time had a different ending. Late in August the Board of Zoning and Appeals found for us and our application by a unanimous vote. The Long Island Commercial Review, in reporting this decision, stated, its belief that the additional facilities provide "a community service unique in character, commendable in purpose and in the public interest of the North Hempstead community."

The experience we had gone through at that hearing I still found difficulty in understanding, despite the fact that I have been at war against prejudice down the long line of years.

My reaction was even deeper because of my faith in the democratic process, my belief in the right of dissent, of lawful and peaceful assembly, of petition. But outrageous conduct in an official community hearing is something quite different. This is not freedom in action—it is destruction of freedom.

In spite of all this, however, all that the experience had done to me personally, nothing could shake me or my colleagues at Human Resources Center in our faith in the democratic way. It may be difficult at times, it may involve a struggle against obstacles of many kinds.

I remain convinced that under our system of a government of law, justice is and will remain available and obtainable for all citizens, regardless of color or creed, or whether they walk on one leg or two.

The lawyer who had led the attack at the first melée before the Town Board, was on hand to announce, immediately after learning of the new verdict by the Zoning and Appeals people, that the case would be appealed to the New York State Supreme Court.

This, of course, would cost a great deal of money. Almost immediately the neighbors began a new door-to-door campaign, whipping up the residents for action. Many gave. They had to stand together now. We're all in this together, friend. We've got to get this money to stop Mr. Viscardi and his plans for his crippled children and his crippled workers and his school.

Early in 1971, the case was heard in Nassau County Supreme Court. Here the rules of judicial courtroom procedure took over; the spectators in the court could have been cited for contempt if they dared to interrupt or disturb the proceedings. The evidence went in the record without interruption. The judge took the matter under advisement. The waiting began again. But the work of our Center went on.

So we would have to bring in our lawyers and our people and we would have to plan to go into the courts of the state to defend ourselves and our plans once again against these people and their charges.

16

A DEGREE OF HONOR

||||||||||||||||||||||||||||||||||||||||||||||||||||||||||||||||||||||||||||||||||||||||||||||||||

In my office at Abilities, a group of young students from the University of Bridgeport, Connecticut, gathered around my desk. In the fashion of the times, some of them were bearded, some of them long haired, but all were neat, clean and obviously deeply in earnest.

They were there for a curious reason. Some time back, previous to that spring day when they arrived at my office, they had been leaders in a demonstration at their university against our military involvement in Southeast Asia. They had demonstrated also in favor of a number of other causes, including the pollution problem, the ecological problem, the racial problem in America and other controversial subjects.

At about that same time, the President and faculty of the university informed me that they wished to award me an honorary degree at their commencement exercises and invited me to make the commencement address to the graduating class and their guests. The chancellor advised me that the students were concerned. Who was this Dr. Viscardi? What did he stand for? What were his attitudes toward today's world problems and toward those young people who themselves would soon begin shouldering more and more of these problems?

The students insisted my speech be relevant to the issues of the day in which they were concerned, he said. They wanted to meet with me to determine my views and what I would say on Viet Nam, Cambodia, war or peace, the population explosion, pollution, freedom, and similar pertinent subjects.

I told the chancellor I would not meet with the students at the university but would provide transportation to our campus for a delegation representing them.

Upon this all agreed.

It was a unique situation—the audience you were about to address asking to look you over first. But that was all right with me. They were not a mob shouting me down. They wanted a chance for a mature face-to-face encounter—in advance. I told them by all means to come.

I found it a moving and exhilarating experience. They listened to me talk about myself, as is my wont, I suppose, surrounded by pictures, honorary degrees, citations from around the world, and framed letters on the walls, the model of my sailboat, mementoes—the whole range of a man's memorabilia.

Because they were obviously sincerely interested, I not only told them about Human Resources Center and our people, I took them on a tour of the Center: the School and its children, the pool, the Abilities workshop with its production lines, the glass-carving operation, the complex of activities and recreational areas, the bowling alley for our workers and students. They saw it all.

Paul Hearne, himself one of the student leaders at Hofstra, was with us, along with Frank Gentile and some of my other colleagues. After our student visitors toured our facilities and we were back in my office, Paul, on his litter, opened the discussion.

"Well, I guess you fellows have been around the school and have seen what the school does to allow kids to go to school," Paul pointed out. "Before this place was around, they didn't have this opportunity, at least I did not have the opportunity. I was tutored at home. I came here in the tenth grade of high school. Before that when I was tutored I had several hours of school a week which probably seems pretty nice . . . but it left a lot of gaps in my education. When I came here, we really got a lot of work done and I started to catch up to my grade level. Then when I went to Hofstra University. . . ."

"I think, Paul," I suggested, "that you should reflect some of your feelings about the Town Board hearing and the neighbors. . . .

Paul, who had stayed through most of the first hearing, gave them a vivid account of the storm and tumult of that day.

"These people, these neighbors," he said, "simply didn't want this building here. They were worried about what we might do to hurt their neighborhood."

"Why would they worry about the neighborhood?" one of the visiting Bridgeport students asked.

"If we could answer that question, maybe we could deal with them rationally," Paul said. "It had to do with a lot of prejudice on their part."

The student persisted, "Couldn't you have brought in a lot of people who support the work you're doing?"

Paul agreed it might have been possible but added: "A lot of this has to do with local politics and local government."

Another student remarked, "Well, isn't it a big enough thing where you might want to organize people to put pressure on the specific council members?"

Strangely, at that moment I found a curious rapport with this other generation. I was the conservative older generation and these were the young college student protesters. I did not agree with many, perhaps most, of their causes and their action programs. I abhor courses of action that include or promote violence. I abhor all who want to tear down this nation in the name of serving it.

And yet, as I talked with them about our problems, about their concerns, I discovered that this group of college liberals who happened *not* to be among those who approved or sought violence, did share some of our basic concern. Not for destruction. Not for bombings. But they were concerned, really concerned, about the elements of our society, which is also their society, theirs now, theirs to inherit.

They were all eating lunch, in my office, sandwiches and coffee, as we talked. They were eager to hear about our problems and our plans. It became interesting and exciting. At one point I told them of suggestions for me to speak at local universities and high schools, run full-page advertisements in local papers, and enlist local universities so that we could stage a real march on North Hempstead Town Hall, purposeful but peaceful, with the college students pushing the wheel chairs.

This they were for. We should be heard, they said. We had to be heard. Because, as one youth put it, there are so many ways you can serve a cause, and so many ways you can reveal what you really are.

One of them asked me, "Do you have any programs where you would allow young people like myself to manage, to become involved in Human Resources Center?"

I explained that we had a summer camp program that ran for four weeks but what we really needed, summer and winter, were male volunteers and the physical help required when we take our children on field trips.

"The reason I mention it," the student explained, "is that sometimes organizations that could use young people's help just don't make any provision to try to get it."

I had a feeling that here, in this youth's indication that he wanted to be part of our activity, that he wanted to play his part here, was an answer, totally unexpected but full of meaning.

"We feel," I told him, "that the whole future lies with the young people. Our whole program is geared to reaching the young, to getting our message across to them, to letting them share with us the things that we are doing."

There was silence for a moment between this youth and myself. "Because if the world I grew up in is going to change," I told them finally, in words that sprang from the depths of my feelings, "you boys are going to change it."

We looked at each other across a chasm of time. But they knew and I knew the truth of what I said.

On May 31st, I made the commencement address at the University of Bridgeport and was awarded the honorary degree of Doctor of Humane Letters. There had been some rumors and reports that the Black Panthers might show up and cause trouble, but nothing of the sort happened.

It was a warm, pleasant typical commencement day on the campus, full of early spring foliage and flowers, with parents and young people mingling amid ivy-covered buildings, and academic pageantry—the black-robed seniors, the faculty, the recipients of honorary degrees, the familiar academic gowns and tasseled caps.

In some of the things I said that day, however, I was talking to those young men who came to see me, and to hundreds like them in that graduating class, much more than I was to the parents, the older set, like myself.

In a talk of this kind, to a large group of youth, I really don't try to pull my punches. You talk to the young in straightforward terms. I told them that all the sacrifices of our work and study and training are worth it, and that the goals in America are great.

It is their testing ground—the road ahead. There

they will prove their stamina, their willingness to face
the difficult decisions in dealing with problems of
prejudice and injustice and all the rest of our difficulties. Would they deal with them not destructively,
wantonly, but build and rebuild those qualities which
truly underlie and sustain the greatness of any nation,
any people?

"This land America . . . has nourished my dreams
and given me the opportunity to be free to seek my
own destiny, not as a crippled man but as one seeking
out the challenges of life; to love and be loved; to be
the same as, not different from, the rest of the world.
In what other land could I have found this opportunity to be free?

"Freedom isn't easy. It takes guts. Some people have
them, some have not. The twentieth century, most
violent crucible yet provided for the human race, is
rapidly finding out which is which.

"In that testing, the great republic of the west
stands supreme. Her freedom is not perfect but it is a
long-sight better than that of any of her contemporar-
ies. Her liberties are not everywhere as thorough and
complete as they should be—but compared to the
laughable mockeries of liberty that go on in Russia
and elsewhere, they shine like a beacon in the night.

"She is awkward at times, our beloved country,
blundering at times. . . . She is, now and again, an
object of ridicule to a carping world and, upon occasion, an object of scorn.

"But, by God, she is free."

I wanted to spell out that first truth, that we could

not, must not forget. And there were other areas, other things, they had to know about what I believed and where I stood. And these other things were important, equally real, equally part of the dream.

". . . There is a high price to be free . . . we must recognize that each of us must give up something to save this nation.

"There is a price to be paid, sacrifices to be made. You and I may have to pay more taxes. The corporation may have to spend more on pollution control. The suburban resident may have to curb his racial prejudices. The worker may have to loosen up access to his union. The military leader may have to give up some of his power. The political leader may have to justify his actions. But remember always that sacrifices are worth the effort to save the land, our land."

All of our life, all of our existence as an institution, beginning with the first pilot plant of Abilities, has been a struggle, a challenge, and we seem to have survived and grown stronger in the face of all these things.

But certain moments sum up our deepest meanings, past or present or future. One such came to me on the occasion of the Commencement of the Human Resources School in the late spring of 1971.

Commencements have their own patterns—patterns of endings and beginnings, of parents and friends and alumni, of hymns and prayers, all the familiar music and words and rituals.

But beneath these, meaning remains. And for me

and for our people at Abilities and the Human Resources School the meaning perhaps went deepest that
spring evening of 1971.

So much was at stake, it seemed to me, as I donned
the academic robe and tasselled cap for this occasion
—our fourth Commencement. So much achieved and
so much still at stake for this student body, for these
seniors and all their graduating dreams as they accepted their diplomas in wheel chairs, on braces and
canes and crutches.

And yet, except for the special character of our
young graduating class of students who only a few
years earlier would never have dared to dream they
could be part of such a graduation, it was like all other
Commencements. We sang "The Star Spangled Ban-
ner" together; Father Robert Gannon, former head of
Fordham University, offered the invocation and gave
the blessing. I said a few words of welcome. And after
that Richard Switzer, Headmaster of our school, in-
troduced William James Caligiuri, one of the top graduating seniors, to make the salutatory remarks.

Extremely handicapped physically, Bill was the re-
cipient of the award for excellence in English and
Social Studies, and had been named a member of the
National Honor Society of Secondary Schools.

This bright and able but still severely crippled
young man did not see himself or his classmates as
different from the hundreds of thousands of other
boys and girls graduating in similar ceremonies across
America that spring. "Tonight," he said, "this graduating class of Human Resources School, like all gradua-

ting classes throughout the nation, is facing a society beset with many problems. What attitude should we take on the war in Viet Nam? On the solution of our ecological problems? On the wisdom of spending millions of dollars on our space program while medical research is crying for aid?"

Bill cited a wide span of other problems ranging from economic and medical to the rising crime rates and above all, drugs.

He was not talking of himself or of the school's special role. He spoke, as most young people speak, of trying to right the wrongs of the world around him.

"Perhaps the major problem with which we will be confronted is the ever increasing drug problem. I believe that our government has not yet really come to grips with this problem. Our government seems reluctant to take the necessary steps to stop the flow of drugs, a business which has become a multibillion dollar enterprise. Let us begin to cut this tree of misery at its roots, instead of letting this rotten fruit pollute our country's young people. . . . It has already caused enough damage by breeding crime and delinquency in our streets."

He went on to plead for more action, for the imposition of economic sanctions against nations who allow the production of drugs in their country for importation into America.

It was a strong and moving statment, startling to many in the audience for its candor and its power.

There were songs, too, sung by the student choral group. And the Associate Commissioner of Education

in New York State, Dr. Philip Langworth, spoke of
the future and its promise and told the young people
of that graduating class, "set your goals as high or
higher than you can ever hope to reach. Do something
in your life that will touch the lives of others—for
good. Continue always to reach for the unreachable
star."

I was deeply touched as I listened to all these words,
so frequently familiar, and still unique and important
for this special class, this special Commencement with
so much, as I knew, still to be resolved. Our class
Valedictorian, Robert Edward Yellen, also a member
of the National Honor Society, spoke not only of the
importance of his generation but of all young people,
handicapped or non-handicapped.

"Our generation can be expected to produce its own
Pasteurs and Salks," he told these parents and friends
and schoolmates. "All of these frontiers remain for
conquering by our generation of high school graduates. Many will actively participate in the field of
medicine, sociology, law enforcement, physics, di-
plomacy, legislation, biology, law and education. The
important point is that no one, no matter how limited
in horizons, should sit by and do nothing."

The world he described was not a world of rejection
of the disabled, even the most severely disabled. It was
a world of participation in which all could play a part
in some significant measure. Our main speaker,
Charles K. Cox, President of the Insurance Company
of North America, supported that view: "It has been
said that there are no great men, or women," he de-

clared in his address, "only ordinary people who achieve greatness by responding to great challenges. And you," he added, to these young graduates," are among them."

In my own closing words to this class and to the student body, the parents and guests, I was able to report good news. We had fought through on several fronts in our struggle with the neighbors to start construction on the new school building. The word had come only the day before from Jack Coffey. "Justice has triumphed," Jack announced. "The appeal of your protesting neighbors to the New York State Supreme Court has been rejected."

I was able to announce this in the brief talk I gave at the closing of that Commencement. I was able to tell them that, although further litigation was pending, the bulldozers were already on the grounds, the digging of the foundation had begun.

It was all true and exciting. Yet we knew that trouble could still lie ahead. There were other legal steps our opponent might take or try to take. We could still be held up, delayed, who knew for how long. But one thing we also knew: The building had begun and in the end we would win, in this land of freedom, because the cause of this school for the extremely disabled child—with the right to a real education—is a part of American freedom and equality.

The conventional thing to have said then, I suppose, would have been to wish them all success and happiness for the rest of their lives, and to assure them of all the certainties about their future and that of the school. But there could be no such certainties, as I fully knew. so instead I wished them something else perhaps even more important:—meaning, underlying meaning that infuses and enriches.

"And meaning is not just something you stumble across like the answer to a riddle or a prize in a treasure hunt," I told this graduating class. "Meaning is something you build into your life, starting fairly early and working at it fairly hard. You build it out of your own chance, out of your affections and loyalties, out of the experience of mankind as it is passed on to you, out of your talent and understanding, out of the things you believe, out of the people you love, out of the values for which you are willing to sacrifice. The ingredients are there. You and I are the only ones who can put them together into that unique pattern that is our lives."

Meaning would be there. The children would be there. The classes. The graduates. Alumni. The dream and the fulfillment.

Freedom to dream, freedom to struggle, freedom to achieve our goals. Freedom to build a new school building for these incredible children, these incredible adults of tomorrow.

Outside, in the cool spring Commencement evening, the bulldozers waited for the morning sun.

INDEX

201